KATE

Billie Virginia Banning

Copyright © 2013 Billie Virginia Banning
All rights reserved.

ISBN: 1483922995
ISBN-13: 9781483922997

Library of Congress Control Number: 2013905541
CreateSpace Independent Publishing Platform
North Charleston, South Carolina

This book is dedicated to the family of Leroy and Katherina Miller

This is the story as remembered by Kate and Billie when Kate was 90 years old and Billie was 70 years old. It may not be quite true.

I want to thank Awesome Annie Booth and Knowledgeable Keegan Gee Taylor for their hard work editing it.

Chapter 1

Daniel entered the room with a little trepidation. This was the first time his family had been at a large gathering with these settlers in Indiana. He always felt uncomfortable until he became acquainted with some of the people. He was lean and hard after working long hours on one farm after another. He had brown eyes and a somber expression. He liked seeing new country, but he was uncomfortable when he was around people he did not know. His family moved often and even though he was twenty-eight years old, he had not found a woman with whom to share his life.

It always seemed to Mose Troyer, Daniel's father, that there were more opportunities somewhere else. The families were not afraid of hard work, and so they would have enough to get them through to the next harvest. They would buy more land in the early spring in a new location. Mose always wanted a lot of land so that his married children would have plenty of room for farms of their own. It was imperative that they planted crops so that they would have the cash from the harvest. It seemed to Daniel that his family had to start over each year.

Because they were Amish, they were welcomed and included in each new Amish settlement and invited to all functions. Still, it was hard for Daniel to make new friends. Mose and his brother, Joe, always made themselves right at home at each new place. Daniel's mother, Catherine, would meet with the other women and discuss child-raising, quilting, gardens, canning, clothes-making and all the other jobs that the women did to hold heart and hearth together. When there was a get-together, Daniel often would stay with the older men rather than the young adults. He liked listening to their talk and no one cared if he said anything or not. As he listened, he continually glanced around the room.

His eyes moved from group to group. Then he saw her. She was tiny. She was in a group talking to other young men and women. She had a shawl around her shoulders which helped to decorate her plain, long dress. As she talked, she moved her hands and smiled often. When others talked, she listened intently. Daniel could not hear what they were saying across the room, but he liked looking at her. It was a vivacious group, but Daniel had no interest in the others. He just watched her from across the room.

As he watched, she turned away from the others. Thoughts sped through Daniel's mind. Was she leaving so early? Who was she? Was she married or promised to someone? How could he find out? Then he grimaced. It really didn't matter. She would have no interest in him anyway. Besides, she was young, probably still in her teens. Just looking at her made Daniel hold his breath. Usually, when Daniel thought of his reticence to talk, he would silently grin. But not now, she would think him so boring.

Daniel watched her as she came toward him. Maybe one of these men was her father. As she came closer, she seemed more and more beautiful. She walked right up to Daniel and held out her hand. "You must be Daniel. I'm Sarah Yoder. Our mothers are first cousins. Welcome to our community."

Daniel took her tiny hand in both of his large ones and just held it. "Hello," he said.

After a minute Sarah gently removed her hand. "Let me introduce you to some of the others."

Daniel meekly followed her. He knew he would follow her anywhere. She led him back to the group of young adults. As he was introduced he would say 'Hello' each time and extend his hand. He had a good head for remembering names, but the only name he remembered that night was Sarah Yoder.

Sarah's parents, Jonathan and Magdelena Miller Yoder, had bought a farm when they married and they owned it still. Over the years they had made many improvements, so it was very nice. They both worked hard and they liked having a nice house. They went places in an elegant one-horse carriage. They had a garden that was one of the most productive in the area. Sarah loved working in the garden and was good at growing things. She also helped to take care of the farm animals; she fed the rabbits and chickens, gathered the eggs, and slopped the pigs. She knew how to quilt. She had also earned a reputation of having great nursing skills. Often when neighbors had a sick child, they would turn to Sarah for help. When Magdelena's legs were covered with sores from an unknown source, Sarah had washed them daily and put oil on them to keep them moist. They had eventually healed.

When Sarah's brother, Manassa, married Lydia, she objected to Sarah living in the house. She thought there were too many adult women there. So, at that time, Sarah had moved in to help her Aunt Mary. Mary had several children and Sarah's help had been needed. Now, however, the baby was getting big enough so that it was not necessary to watch him every minute and she was not really necessary.

The Troyers were roamers. They too worked hard. But the grass was always greener somewhere else. They often moved. As a result, they did not have things nearly as nice as Sarah's parents. Often they did not get back the money they had put into a place. But when Mose was ready to move, his children and their families would usually move with him. Often they would ship their accumulation of things by rail. This time they had shipped a carload of machinery and household goods, a carload of livestock, and a carload of lumber.

Sarah was outgoing and friendly. Daniel was a quiet, gentle man. Daniel's father watched the young woman and his son. It seemed as though Daniel thought she was wonderful. On the way home Mose said, "That Sarah sure is a flirt. You spent a lot of time with her. Don't you go getting stuck on her."

Daniel looked at his mother then back at his dad, "Her mother, Magdelena, is Mama's first cousin." he said.

His mother smiled a tiny smile and turned her face away from her husband. Daniel and Sarah soon became a couple. Before long they had decided to get married. Mose grumbled but could see that there was no point in opposing the marriage. On a cool day in March in the year 1906, they were married. The Troyers had come from North Dakota where the family had been living.

Chapter 2

Soon after the marriage of Daniel and Sarah, Mose decided to move to Michigan, where many of the Troyers were living. So Sarah said goodbye to the only place she had ever lived and moved with Mose and Catherine and their other children. She promised herself that she would not cry. Daniel would do his best and it was the husband that made the decisions. She knew she loved him and he loved her.

They moved to White Cloud, Michigan. Once again they found places for the families to live. They planted crops and worked hard. The women had huge gardens and during the summer and fall they had fresh fruits and vegetables. The families wasted none of the food. Anything that was too plentiful to eat fresh was canned and saved for winter.

Sarah worked hard but she did not feel especially accepted by the other women. They had been together for years and she often felt left out as they talked about times they had had. She had bouts of homesickness. Then in September of 1906, she started having trouble keeping her food down. When she realized she was going to have a baby, she dearly missed her own mother.

Sarah and Daniel's first child, Lena, was born on May 16, 1907. Sarah kept Lena with her as she continued working in the garden, cooking meals, doing laundry, and cleaning the house. Lena was a lot of work, but Sarah loved her baby.

In the fall of that year, once again she had morning sickness. On April 24, 1908 Mose was born. Daniel was happy that this time he had a son.

Soon after Mose was born, many of the Troyers left Michigan by an immigrant train and went to Kansas. Again the families combined their possessions and shipped two carloads by rail; one of machinery and one carload was livestock and household goods mixed. Sarah and Daniel decided to stay in Michigan. After a year, the Kansas Troyers moved again to Colorado because homestead land was available.

On October 16, 1909, Sarah and Daniel's third child, Katherina, was born in White Cloud, Michigan. Her sister, Lena, had turned two in May and her brother, Mose, had turned one in April. When Kate was three weeks old, Daniel decided to yield to the urgings of his brothers and sisters and the family began packing so that they could move to Colorado,

So with a two-year-old and a one-year-old and a very young baby, they climbed into a wagon and set out for the new and better land. Daniel's relatives had written about the wonderful land for the taking. They stopped in Indiana to see Sarah's parents and other relatives. Kate for her part decided to go along. She clung to her mother in fear of a minute of desertion.

From Indiana they decided to go by train. It would be an adventure. It was supposed to be easier. It took three weeks by train to get to Colorado, where the Troyer relatives lived. The train was boring for the two toddlers. Kate was by far the best traveler of the lot. She slept and nursed and continued to cling to her mother. The rest of the family was careful of the food they had brought and would only eat small amounts at a time. Daniel and Sarah told the two older children Bible stories and tried to interest them in the changes of scenery. When the trip was over and they arrived to be met by Daniel's father, Mose, it was indeed a relief to get off the train. Also, in the vicinity were three of Daniel's married brothers and their wives, two of his sisters and their husbands, and his brother Joe, a bachelor.

Daniel's brothers had written to him and convinced him to move to Colorado because of all the free land. The best land was taken by the time they arrived. The land where Sarah and Daniel homesteaded was very poor farm land. Water was deep everywhere but Daniel was a dowser and Sarah convinced him to look for water. So Daniel took a piece of wire that was leftover from the clothesline wire. He bent it so that it looked like an outline of a western hat. He held the wire by the brim part of the hat with his palms up and started walking their land. He walked and walked but there was no water to be found. Land without water had no value so it went back to the government. Uncle Joe's land also was without water and it too was returned to the government.

Chapter 3

When they first arrived in Colorado, the family moved into the house that Mose and Catherine had built when they first came. It was very small but had served as a home while they had built a larger, nicer home. Now, once again, it was a temporary home while Dan and Sarah decided where they would settle.

Uncle Joe and Daniel went looking at the land still available. They each found a half section with water that they would buy. Daniel had money from the sale of crops and land in Michigan. This time when Daniel doused for water he found some near the surface of the land and not too far from a good location for a house.

The families had come because there was homestead land available. In order to keep the land, they had to build a house on it within a year. Each family had been given one-fourth of a section. Joe and Daniel's land was not homestead land as they had each bought a half section.

After he paid for his half section, his brothers' families helped Daniel and Sarah build a two-story house on it. The house was painted gray. The children would sleep upstairs. They also built a chicken house, a barn for the horses and cows, and a shed. The home had water nearby. It had a hand pump and a windmill. When the wind didn't blow then water was hand pumped.

When Kate was just a small child, long before she started school, she would go out and pump water by hand and carry the bucket carefully into the house. Water was precious. She was always careful because she did not want to do the job twice. Young Mose often went to work in the fields with his dad. Lena and Kate helped in and around the house. One of Kate's earliest jobs was pulling weeds. Lena loved to clean house. Kate loved to be outside. Weeding wasn't a favorite job but it did give her an opportunity to be outside for long periods of time. She also liked examining the garden on a daily basis to see the changes to the plants as they punched their way up to the surface and then continued growing. She liked it when the blossoms first appeared on the trees and she could hardly wait until the fruit first formed in a blossom.

Soon after Kate turned two, Edna was born. Edna did spend lots of time lying in bed during the day because Mama had so much work to do, but in the evenings, Mama would rock and hold Edna and sing little songs to her. Kate and Lena and Mose would entertain themselves. Lena and Kate were close friends. Mose liked to play alone. When Edna was two, Perry was born. Now Mama would hold Edna and Perry in the evenings. As Perry began sitting up, he and Edna became good friends. They would play together during the day.

Sarah called the water hard. That would make Kate smile. But her mom would put a water softener into the water to wash clothes. They would use strong soap to wash dishes, which they washed in a dish pan. Kate or one of the other children would bring in the water and Sarah would heat it on the stove while they were eating supper. Kate would stand on a box to wash dishes because she could not reach the counter. She and Lena would wash and dry. Mama would put them away and clean up the kitchen after cooking the meals on a coal stove.

Sarah had six babies in about nine years. Lyman was born on May 14, 1916. Perry had just turned three. Sarah, or one of the children, pumped her own wash and scrubbing water. She made all their clothes, and cooked on a coal stove. Coal burning in a stove can be a slow, smoky, contrary fire. There were always diapers hanging on the clothesline. Not once did Sarah ever say that she had too much work to do. When she walked, Sarah took very small steps but she took them very fast.

She also hatched baby chicks, either in an incubator or under hens. She always had a beautiful garden. Daniel would plow the garden and get water to it, via pipes and hose. She had strawberries all summer long. She grew peas, corn, green beans, cabbage, squash, onions and lettuce. Kate would often end up hoeing weeds out of the garden. It was her least favorite garden job.

Watching chickens hatch was wonderful. Nearly always for the first hatching, Sarah would have Kate go with her to look because she knew that Kate loved it so. Sarah would put about 140 eggs at a time in the incubator. She and Kate would turn them gently for twenty-one days. Then on the twenty-first day Sarah would say, "Kate, do you want to see the chicks?" She and Kate would head to the incubator and pull up the tray and there would be over 100 baby chicks; little, yellow, fluffy things. They would seem happy and did not act the least bit scared. That was always a real joy.

Lena was two and a half years older than Kate. She was an inquisitive girl, but she cared not for baby chicks, or gardens, or getting eggs. She liked to clean house, take care of the babies, and listen to older women talk.

Kate always wanted to play. She loved the outdoors. After thrashing wheat they'd have stacks of fresh straw and she loved lying on her back in the straw, watching the wonderful, white floating clouds. Oh, it felt so good! When she was with a sister or brother it was great fun to jump into the hay stacks. Sometimes they played tag or hide-and-seek. Kate was one of the fastest runners and she loved to run.

Mama and Papa had taken the very small bedroom on the first floor and the six children shared the upstairs room. As you went upstairs, Mose and Perry slept to the right of the stairs in a small area. Then to the left there was a bigger space with two double beds. Lena and Edna shared one bed and Lyman slept with Kate. Kate would rub his feet in the winter to help keep them warm until he went to sleep. Sometimes she could hear Lena and Edna whispering but most of the time, it was too quiet for her to hear the words. It really didn't matter. By the time she went to bed, Kate was ready to go to sleep.

Chapter 4

Kate was glad when she was, at last, old enough to go to school. But she was nervous, too. The Troyer families spoke Pennsylvania Dutch at home. Kate had learned some English words from Lena when they played school or were playing away from the adults. But when they were with the rest of the family they would talk in 'the old way'. They seldom saw anyone except family and they all spoke Pennsylvania Dutch. Kate was very shy and seldom talked to grown-ups that were not related. At school she spoke only when the teacher would ask her a question. She was always good at school and listened carefully. Even though she did not know much English when she started school, she learned the alphabet quickly. She was fascinated that those twenty-six letters could go together and make thousands of words. It was a kind of magic.

After Kate started school, sometimes Mama would need Kate to stay home from school and take care of Lyman. Lyman cried a lot. Kate's ears would bother her so she would often wear a scarf. At first, she thought that Lyman must have earaches, too. But after watching him she decided that he was having headaches. Perry and Edna were very good about playing together so they didn't need much watching.

Kate missed a lot of school but school was not hard for her. She was always good for her teacher and the teacher would be nice to her. But sometimes she thought that was a problem too. Sometimes the other kids would call her 'goody-two-shoes.' As with many shy people, the other children thought she was stuck up.

Since going to school, she now had books to read. At home there were no books but the Bible. As the boys got older they sometimes would sneak a book into the house. Occasionally, when Kate made their beds she would find one by Zane Grey or James Fennimore Cooper and get to read it in bits and pieces but most of the time at home she did not have much time to read anyway. Papa didn't approve of reading stories. He would say, "What if the Lord would come and I was reading a story? He'd go right on past me."

To go to school, Lena would hitch up the horse to the buggy. Then she would drive the buggy the two and one-third miles and Mose and Kate would ride. At noon, it was Lena's job to feed and water the horse that was tied to a post, patiently waiting for the return trip. Their papa had to pay tuition for them to go to Limon School. They lived across the county line. Limon was in Lincoln County and their farm was in Elbert County. It was sixteen miles to Matheson School.

When Kate was in third grade, Grandpa Troyer donated land for a school house. It was called the Troyer School. It was one and a half miles by road from Papa's house and Kate and her brother and sisters walked. They would cut across the fields and save many steps. It was a one-room school. There were all eight grades in the one room, with seventeen or eighteen students at one time. Many of the students were Kate's cousins.

Chapter 5

Kate liked working alone in the garden. It was so wonderful to feel the dirt between her fingers and toes and how she liked seeing the plants growing, knowing that they would provide food for her family. It was rather nice being away from everyone. Often Lymon was with her since he had been old enough to get around. Sometimes she had to keep an eye on Perry and Edna, too. Once in a while, she wished she were more like Lena. Lena was so out- going. Everyone liked her. Edna really didn't seem to care whether people liked her or not. She did just as she pleased. She didn't work as hard as Lena and Kate. Mama seemed to favor her. But of course, she was only six and had frequent bouts of tonsillitis. Kate was almost nine years old.

Kate lived in an Amish community of seven other families. One of the adults in five of the families was another child of Grandpa Moses. So Kate had lots of cousins living close. They would see each other at church every Sunday and they also had gatherings at night. Amish people were taught that the way of life was to work hard and this was the life that all the families followed.

Kate would often let her mind wander while working in the garden and she would think about things she had experienced. Sometimes she would think of her Grandma Catherine who lived nearby. Grandma was a quiet woman because that was how Grandpa Troyer wanted her to be. She worked hard as did all the Amish people of the community. Sometimes she would silently smile when she agreed with something the children did, when she knew Grandpa would not approve but she could see no harm. Grandpa thought children should be seen and not heard. Grandma liked to listen to the children when they were with her alone. Grandpa thought children should always be busy working. Grandma liked to see them stop working to dream or take a little time to play.

Chapter 6

One morning Grandpa Troyer came to the house. Grandma was sick and he was going to take her to the Mennonite hospital in La Junta. While she was in the hospital, Catherine heard the story of salvation. All you had to do was believe that Jesus was the Son of God and that he had died on the cross for your sins. If you would just ask Him to come into your heart and to forgive your sins, He would. Grandma Troyer died August 8, 1918.

After the funeral, preachers from La Junta came to the Amish settlement to preach the gospel of Christ. Mama, Uncle Joe, and Grandpa Mose accepted the Lord Jesus as their Savior. Kate believed the first time she heard the story of salvation. She felt the Holy Spirit come over her and she never doubted that this was the true way to heaven. She liked the new God she learned about. He was a God of love. He was a God that came to save the world from sin. He was a God that was her redeemer. He was a God that did not expect her to work her way to heaven.

The Amish read and studied only the Old Testament and they continued to meet on Sundays. So Grandpa and Uncle Joe began to study the New Testament on Monday evenings. The family went to both meetings. The Monday evening group continued to grow and they began meeting in the schoolhouse. Slowly many members of the community began to believe the New Testament as well as the Old Testament. The Amish community slowly became a Mennonite community.

After a year had passed, Mose and Lena were to get baptized. Kate went to Mama, "Mama, I want to get baptized, too.'

Mama said, "Oh, Kate, you're just too young to understand."

Kate said, "No, I'm not, Mama. I have Jesus as my Savior. I want to get baptized."

Papa had been listening, "Kate, you're too young to understand. You can get baptized later." And so, when Lena and Mose were baptized, Kate was sitting with the rest of the family.

After Sarah accepted Jesus as her Savior, she was very concerned for her parents and other family members back in Indiana. She had to tell them the story of salvation.

She wrote countless letters to her relatives who were Amish.

Papa said, "If you mail those letters, they will shun you. You will never be able to go home again."

Mama said, "I have to tell them. They don't know. They need to know. They won't be saved." She wrote and mailed the letters.

Mama did make a trip back home to visit her parents. Some of the people in the community were not happy to see her, but her mom and dad were. They listened to the story. They began to read the New Testament. The Amish were still waiting for the Savior to come. As they read the New Testament and saw how the prophecies were fulfilled, they came to believe that Jesus was the Savior.

When Mama's Mother died, Sarah's father wanted her to go home for the funeral. But Sarah decided not to go. She knew that many family members were upset because she said the New Testament was true. She was afraid that there would be controversy at her mother's funeral. Her father was very disappointed that she did not come. When her father died, she decided to go to his funeral. She was getting ready when she heard a voice saying to her so clearly, "Your dad wanted you to go to your mother's funeral and you would not go. You will not go to your dad's funeral."

Sarah went to her husband and said, "Daniel, I'm not going to my dad's funeral. I heard a voice and it told me I would not go."

Daniel said, "You might decide to go. Go ahead and get ready."

So Sarah packed her clothes and made arrangements to go. Right before she left she noticed that Daniel was not well. He said, "Go ahead. I'll be all right."

Sarah stayed. It was a good thing because Daniel had double pneumonia and would probably have died without her constant care. Mama was always doing things like that. She often nursed the neighbors when they were in poor health. She helped deliver babies. Seldom did the people feel that they could afford the doctor in Limon and she just seemed to know what to do to make them feel better.

Chapter 7

Soon after the baptisms, Kate came home from school and found the house in a shambles. Sarah and Daniel had decided to move to Colorado Springs. The past winter was hard on Papa. He dreaded the long hours in the fields. They hoped that life would be easier in the city. Mama would not have to go out and milk the cows before and after working in the house and garden all day. They would move into a house with room for a garden and a few chickens. Daniel would use his big truck and make deliveries.

Kate hated to move away from the friends and family she had lived by all her life. Lena looked forward to moving to the city. Mose hoped he would have a little free time after school instead of going out and working in the field with his dad.

When Grandma had died, GrandpaTroyer had moved into his daughter Mary's house. He stayed for a while but he did not like it. One day he said, "I'm not staying here any longer." His children got together and moved him into the little house that he and grandma lived in when they first moved to Colorado. His son, Christian, and his family moved into the big house up in front. It was understood that Christian's wife, Elizabeth, would take care of Grandpa. She did take care of him while Daniel and Sarah lived in Colorado Springs.

For work, Daniel had to find people who needed something delivered. Sometimes he would go far distances. Then he would look for something to bring back near home. Sometimes he would be gone two or three days. He and Mama were sorry about the absences. They had thought that by moving to the city he would be home every night, but it had not worked out that way.

Papa had been bothered by asthma for many years. Now he found that he had sugar diabetes, too. He needed insulin to control it. Sometimes he would be so weak he would not make the deliveries when he said he would. When he was home, Mama gave him the insulin shots. When he was away from home, he would have to give them to himself. He hated that. He would put it off sometimes until it was really too long and he would fall asleep. Then he would make another late delivery.

Mama worried when Papa was on the road. They talked about it and Papa quit deliveries unless they were just around Colorado Springs and Manitou Springs. If he could not make it home that night, he would turn down the delivery. If he had no deliveries, he would pick up fruit down by the river and go from house to house selling it. They were not making a lot of money this way either. They did not have a cow, so sometimes they did not have milk at every meal. It was sorely missed.

When they moved to Colorado Springs, the nation was in the First World War. The other children tormented the Troyer children, often calling them names and making fun of them. Kate did not understand about the war that was across the ocean and could not understand the other children heckling her and her sisters and brothers.

After a trying day at school, Kate went to her mom, "Mama, why do the kids make so much fun of us?"

"I'm sorry, Kate, it is because our ancestors were from Germany. It has been many years since my Grandmother and Grandfather came to America, but we like many of the old ways. Now that the United States is at war with Germany, I'm afraid my children are in for an unpleasant time."

"What can we do, Mama?"

"We can't change the way we are. I am going to pray about this and I think maybe it will be a good idea for you to take this problem to God. We are going to continue to be kind to our neighbors and not bear them any ill will. People are the way they are. We just have to keep acting the way we know is right."

Kate sighed, "It's hard, Mama. It's good that I have Lena to play with me."

Chapter 8

One day Christian called and asked them to come home and take care of Grandpa. They would move into the big house in front and Grandpa would continue to live in the little house in the back. Living in Colorado Springs had not been as successful and easy as they had hoped, so after talking it over, back to the farm they went.

Soon after they moved into the big house, the name 'KATE' was written on many places in the house. Mama was seldom cross but she called Kate and scolded her for writing on the walls and banister of the stairs.

"But, Mama, I didn't do it." Kate said.

"Oh, Kate," said Mama, "Who else would write your name everywhere?"

"I didn't do it." Kate insisted.

"You need to get some soapy water and wash your name off now." Mama said.

This happened periodically over the first year they lived in the house. Each time Kate would be scolded and told to clean off the writing. Each time Kate insisted she had not done it. Each time Kate would be told to wash her name off everywhere.

One time as Kate was washing off her name, she was really angry. She was more upset for being blamed for something she didn't do than she was at all the extra work she had to do. Scrubbing off her name was not an easy task. She noticed that Mama was standing watching her work. Lena saw them and went and stood by Mama.

After a minute, Lena blurted out, "It was Edna, Mama. Edna wrote Kate's name."

Kate heard her and smiled. She kept washing. At least now Mama knew she didn't do it. Then she felt sad. "How come Edna likes to get me into trouble?" she wondered. Her name did not appear on the walls anymore.

Lena loved housework, so she spent most of her time indoors. She dusted, washed windows, and swept. She enjoyed making the house shine. Kate would help her with the morning dishes and then she would head outside to feed the calves and chickens and go work in the garden. Much of the time she would have Lyman with her. She would work there for a couple of hours then it would be time to help with lunch. Mama would cook and then set a big kettle on the stove. The water would heat while they were eating so there was hot water to do dishes. Lena and Kate would do dishes. They traded off washing and drying them. When she had first started at the age of five, those dishes would seem to have a life of their own. Quite often one would slip out of her hands and break into about a thousand pieces, but Kate hardly broke any now.

One task that Kate enjoyed was to go after the milk cows, because it was just walking across that lovely prairie. As she walked, she would look for bird nests and baby rabbits in the spring. Also, there were so many small flowers. Her favorites were the tiny lavender flowers. Sometimes she would pick the dainty lilies. They'd always be completely wilted before she would get home, but the smell would last and last. She would also watch for prairie dog holes. It was always fun trying to sneak up on a prairie dog sitting by its hole. They would suddenly disappear into the hole before she got too close but she could get quite close to the colonies, where several animals would be sitting eight to ten inches tall on their hind legs. She never saw any of them look at her but all at once they scrambled for their holes. They always made her smile.

The farm house was on a small hill with good open views of the plains. There was lots of water when it rained. Usually, they did not have to conserve water. She could see Pike's Peak from the farm.

Nobody worked as hard as Mama. She did most of the meal preparation and supervised what any of the children did. She had a huge garden and lots of chickens. It was her job to do the milking twice a day. She would carry the milk down into the basement to the separator. Whenever they would run out of butter, Mama would put cream into the churn. It was monotonous so the children would take turns and churn and churn and churn, but how great the butter tasted and there was also fresh buttermilk on those days. Lots of times Kate and sometimes Mose, helped with the milking. Kate liked milking the cows, except when there was a heifer that had never been milked. Often she was the one that milked the new heifers. Then she was in danger of being kicked. She must have had a knack though. Maybe it was because she would sing as she milked. She always thought the cows liked her singing. It seemed to her that they stood much quieter while she was singing. Eventually, every heifer seemed to like being milked.

Chapter 9

It took most of two days to do the washing and ironing. It seemed like there were diapers hanging on the clotheslines most days ever since Kate had been born. And when she thought about it, probably even before that, because Mose and Lena weren't that much older than she was.

Kate did like sewing and it was very exciting when Mama would have some material so she could make a new dress. Mama would study the styles and make the dresses different. Kate's favorite dress was a navy blue middy blouse and pleated skirt. How titillating to see a piece of material turn into a dress. Mama had a treadle sewing machine and made the pants for the boys, too. Even after it was dark Mama would be quilting or working on a comforter or sewing clothes for one member of the family or another. Lena and Edna would ask Mama for new clothes and Kate did not seem that eager, so they would get two new dresses for Kate's one. Mostly, Kate had three dresses to wear to school. She would wear her dresses two days in a row. When she got home from school, she changed into work clothes that were really just clothes that were too old to wear away from home. As her dresses would get a little older she might get a new Sunday dress. But most of the time she would wear her Sunday dress to school on Monday.

Lena and Edna would wear a different dress everyday of the week. But week after week they would wear the same clothes. Sometimes Lena would see a friend wear a dress to church and then she would not see it for several weeks. Wouldn't it be wonderful to have so many different clothes? But, of course, that would never happen and besides, where would she keep them? They hardly had storage for the few clothes they had. Kate, on the other hand, was uncomfortable in a new dress. She always had to be so careful not to get it dirty. She preferred the play clothes. She was much more comfortable in them. Lena and Edna loved to get new dresses.

Sometimes Mama would buy material to make Kate a new dress and end up making Lena or Edna one instead. Then Mama would say, "We'll make you one next time, Kate."

Kate would answer, "It's okay, Mama, I like my dresses I wear to school just fine." But she did know that her dresses were not as nice as her sisters' dresses. All of the children knew they had to take care of their clothes and if they did outgrow them before they were worn out, their younger brothers and sisters would wear them.

Mama did make Kate a khaki tent dress. When she put on the new dress, Mama had her picture taken. Kate was so happy. This was very unusual, because Mennonites seldom had their pictures taken.

Mama usually was in the process of making a quilt or a comforter. The tops of both were pieced together with all different colors of material. The comforters were made from old suits and other heavy clothing that the children had outgrown or Papa had worn out. These were tied. Mama would go down and up through the three layers of cloth and then tie a square knot.

Mama would make both quilts and comforters three layers. Whatever she would be working on would be in a frame. If she was not working on it, she would lean it up against the wall. As Lena and Kate became teenagers they would sit and quilt, also. Kate tried so hard but Mama's stitches were much smaller and closer together than those of her daughters. It took much less skill to work on a comforter.

Whenever Mama made clothes she would always save every little scrap. Then if there was time she would begin piecing together a quilt. Kate liked to watch sewing but she loved watching Mama piecing together a quilt. How she would like cutting the small shapes and putting them together to make the beautiful designs. It was so exciting to think that those small pieces of material could be made into the lovely quilts that people had. It was fun looking at the scraps and remembering the clothes that they came from. And after the top was pieced together it would be put with two other pieces of material to make a warm cover for a bed. It took a long time to make one quilt because of the thousands of tiny hand-sewn stitches.

Mama made Lena a beautiful dress to wear at a wedding of one of her friends at the church. When the visiting preacher came to the house, Lena called down to Mama, "Which dress should I wear for the wedding, the blue one or the rose colored one?"

Mama was just a little shook up. There was no rose dress. Then she called back, "Maybe you should wear the blue one."

"All right, I will." Lena answered.

Chapter 10

Kate was ill one day and had leaned against the wall behind the stove. It was warm there and she was often cold. Her mama and papa were talking in soft tones. Kate did not listen at first and then she heard the word Christmas. After that she strained her ears listening.

Mama said, "We just have to buy the children something for Christmas."

Papa said, "Getting gifts at Christmas is just a bunch of nonsense."

"Please," Mama said, "I want to give them a little something. I have saved a little from my egg money to get them something."

Papa didn't say no. He just grumbled, "It's a bunch of nonsense."

Christmas morning came. Sure enough, when Kate went down to breakfast, the table was set just perfect and on every plate there was a little gift. Kate's was a tablet and pencil. They had all hung stockings and these were filled with fruits and nuts. She was so happy with Mama. Usually, when Papa said something, Mama would just go along. It was great that Mama had stood up to him and made Christmas special. Kate knew that Christmas was a celebration of the birth of Jesus. But it was nice to get a little gift on that morning.

In later years, Kate thought, "Probably this is what happened every year and Mama always made sure we got some little gift and special things to eat."

Chapter 11

Papa only kept a share of what he made. He always had to pay for the bills that had accumulated over the cold winter months. Mama always canned things from the garden but flour and coffee and sugar and oatmeal always had to be bought at the store and sometimes they would run out of other things. They would separate the milk and sell the cream. Mama would trade eggs for store items. At the end of the harvest they would stock up on things to get them through the winter months when things didn't grow.

One day a man from the dairy called. Someone had found a mouse in the cream. They would not buy the cream anymore.

Sunday there was not as much work, but many hours were spent at church. Cows still had to be milked and all the animals had to be fed. Often Sunday's noon meal was fixed on Saturday. It was a time of fellowship with other families that lived close by. The Amish and Mennonites both believed that no unnecessary work was to be done on the Lord's day.

Grandpa decided that Papa should buy the farm and told him how much he wanted for it.

Mama said, "He wants too much money."

Papa said, "He's my father," So he agreed to pay the exorbitant sum.

Papa worked hard. The soil was poor and sometimes there would not be enough water. Then the rains would come and the ground would be muddy and it would be hard to get around. Mose would work in the field with his dad. He also helped to feed the animals.

The girls would help Mama keep the house clean, make the morning and evening meals, pack lunches, do their homework, wash dishes and clothes, and iron the clothes. They also helped with the picking and canning of the fresh vegetables from the garden. Once again they had a cow that had to be milked morning and evening. Butter had to be churned. Bread and cornbread were made from scratch and cooked in a coal stove. It seemed like the work never did get done. Kate and Lena almost always had to do the supper dishes because Edna would head for the outhouse when it was time to wash the dishes and come in just as they were finishing.

Mama would always say, "Just go ahead and get started. There's no sense in just sitting around." So they would start and finish before Edna would get back.

After supper dishes, in the winter, they would do homework or play school until bedtime. Sometimes in the cold winter nights, they would play checkers or card games. Since animals had to be fed and chores had to be done before school, they would get up early, and they would usually be in bed by eight o'clock on school nights.

Often Uncle Joe would come for supper and sit with Grandpa Mose and Daniel in the evenings. He was a bachelor and lived alone. His sisters and Sarah would wash his clothes and cook for him. Sometimes Lyman would go over to Uncle Joe's chair and wait for Uncle

Joe to pick him up. Before long the tickling would start. How Lyman would wiggle and giggle and throw himself around. Katie could remember when he had tickled her. She had hated it, and would steel herself so Uncle Joe thought she was not ticklish. Sometimes she would hide when she saw Uncle Joe coming. She really wanted to just sit on his lap and lean back against his chest. She made a promise to herself: 'No one will ever tickle one of my children.'

Chapter 12

Since they had moved into the house by Grandpa Troyer, he would walk from his house and eat meals with them. After supper he would go sit in the living room and he and Papa would talk. Mostly, Grandpa would talk and Papa would listen. Grandpa always said, "Children should be seen and not heard." The children knew not to make much noise. If it wasn't too cold they would go outside and play.

Kate loved the Colorado night sky. How the moon and stars would shine. After a few minutes outside they could see well enough to get around. Pretty soon, Mama would call, "Bedtime." Then they would all go in and head upstairs.

If Grandpa got sick, Mama would carry his meals to his little house and check on him several times a day. Those days, Kate would have to stay home from school and look after the little ones.

Mama's people sent her a big box of fruit. How the children gathered around that box. Probably enough fruit so they could have as much as they wanted. Kate's mouth was watering. Before the children even got one, Grandpa was there claiming the box for all his children and their families. Instead of several fruits, Kate got one delicious apple.

Mama got quite an inheritance when her parents died. Once again, Grandpa, the patriarch, took most of it and divided it among all his children. Papa did build a water tank and have water piped into the house. He also bought Mama a Holm's Kitchen Range.

One day Grandpa came driving up in a car. How he loved that vehicle. Away he'd go. He was not an especially good driver and he thought he should go as fast as his car could go. Even though the roads had ruts or the railroad tracks were higher than the road, he never slowed down. How passengers would bounce while riding with Grandpa.

He was often getting stuck on the muddy roads. There was a good neighbor that pulled him out more than once. But nothing seemed to slow him down or change his driving habits.

One day, Grandpa came in and ate breakfast as usual. "I'm going to Colorado Springs in my car. I'll be back tomorrow." He got into his car and left.

The next day, there was no Grandpa. A day later, there was no Grandpa. Mama and Papa were so worried. They had a phone but had no idea who they should call. Mama and Papa were so upset at meal times that they would hardly talk at all. After supper they sat in the living room talking in hushed tones, wondering what had happened to Grandpa. Then the phone rang. The voice on the other end of the line said, "Is this Moses Troyer's house?"

Papa said, "Yes, this is his son."

The voice said, "Mr. Troyer was in a car wreck up here in Payton."

Papa said, "Where is he? Was he hurt?"

The voice belonged to a hospital employee, "He was stunned. We had him here overnight. He seems to be all right now. However, he rolled his car and it no longer has a top."

Papa asked, "Should I come and get him?"

There was a pause. Papa looked at Mama and raised his eyebrows. Then he heard his father on the phone, "No, you don't have to come and get me. My car and I are coming home. We don't need any help." And he hung up the phone.

Sure enough that evening, here came Grandpa. His car was dented up and the top was destroyed. But it was running just fine. Grandpa said, "I like it better without a top."

Chapter 13

The years went by. Day followed day. Every day was spent working. But there were good moments. One of the most exciting was when a ford touring car pulled into the yard. Everyone went out to see who it was. Kate hung back but she kept her eyes open. Suddenly, children began climbing out of the car windows. Kate had to grin. It was so funny watching them as they would swing their legs out of the windows and then jump down. Driving the car was Reverend Lewis Miller and riding beside him was his wife, Susie. Susie was carrying a very young son named Robert. Mr. and Mrs. Miller opened the doors when they got out. They were the new neighbors. They had bought the land next door. They really seemed nice.

The oldest boy was Leroy and his brother Frank was not even two years younger than he was. They were obviously happy to be out of the car. When Leroy got out of the car, he looked around. Perry was about his size. Leroy walked over to him and said, "Want to fight?" Perry just shook his head no. The oldest girl in the car was Florence. She was about eight years old. She helped her little brother, Jerry, out of the window. The last one out was Don. He was six years old.

While they were still there, a big truck pulled in behind the car. It was driven by Susie's Brother, Vernon

Unzicker. It was carrying the Miller possessions. One more girl was in the truck. Lena went over to her right away and started talking to her. Kate hung back but slid closer to listen. Her name was Mary and she was just about a year older than Kate. She would turn fourteen before Kate, but this year they had both become teenagers. How Kate hoped that she would have a friend living nearby. It would be wonderful to have friendly neighbors. Kate hung back and kept looking at her feet. But her ears were open. Sarah was just walking up with a bucket of milk fresh from the cow. She sent Lena and Kate into the house for glasses and everyone had a nice glass of warm milk.

The Millers had moved from the town of Tuleta, Texas. Reverend Lewis Miller had been a school teacher but had gone back to school to become an ordained preacher. Mennonites did not pay their ministers. He had come to Limon to start a new Mennonite church. Susie Miller had her nursing degree. They would farm but Reverend Miller would teach school and preach on Sunday. How Kate hoped she would like him.

The Millers and the Troyers did become friendly, especially the children. Their houses were only about a mile apart. They all went to the same church on Sundays. Reverend Miller was a good preacher and a good teacher. Kate was pleased that she knew the family so well. Reverend Miller called her Katie instead of Kate. She liked having a special name when he talked to her.

After the Millers came to Limon, Mama said to Kate one day, "Kate, you've never been baptized. Don't you think you should do that?"

Kate thought about all those people looking at her. She would like to be baptized but now she did not want everyone looking at her. "No, I don't think I will."

Now Mama became concerned. She talked to Reverend Miller and he went over to talk to Kate. "You know Jesus wants you to be baptized."

Kate said, "I accepted Jesus as my Savior a long time ago. I couldn't get baptized then. Why should I get baptized now?"

Reverend Miller smiled at her, "I want you to pray about this."

Kate knew it was past time for her to get baptized so the following Sunday Reverend Miller baptized her.

Mary did become Lena's and Kate's good friend, but Leroy also became a special pal. For some reason, Kate was not shy around Roy. She loved it that he showed off for her and would often make her laugh. In the evenings the children would play kick the can, or hide-and-seek, or different games with balls.

When Kate was twelve, Sarah had had another boy. He was named Daniel after his dad. Sarah really enjoyed this baby. Her other children were in school and she was in the house alone with Daniel during the day. She had learned a lot while raising the other children. When children cried around Dan he would 'give them something to cry about' and swat them on their seats. Sarah tried her best to keep Danny from crying. At the first sign, she would pick him up and coddle him. When Dan was in the house, she would break off small pieces of chocolate and slip them into his mouth.

When Danny was little he slept in his own bed in his parent's bedroom. As he got older, he began sleep walking. So Sarah insisted that his bigger bed be put into their room also. She would wake up as he got out of bed and sing him back to sleep. Daniel thought he should sleep in a room with other children, but Sarah was adamant. She was afraid of where Danny would go when he was sleep-walking.

During the day, before and after school, Lyman and Danny would follow Kate around as she did chores; feeding the chickens and calves, gathering eggs, and working in the garden.

Chapter 14

One day Dan said to Sarah, "I think I'll have Kate run the cultivator."

Sarah said, "You know that if Kate sees a rabbit nest, she'll drive the cultivator around it. We might have some very curvy rows of corn."

Dan frowned, "She'd better not."

Sure enough, Kate was to drive the cultivator. Kate had heard their conversation and knew she was to cultivate in straight rows. So when she came to a rabbit nest or bird nest and saw it in time, she would stop the cultivator, get down, move the nest, drive past, stop and go back and put the nest where it had been. Then she would continue on her way until the next time she saw a nest.

One weekend, when Kate and Leroy were 15 years old, he said to her at church, "I'm going to ask my Pop if he will let me have the car to drive you home. Don't leave, I'll be right back."

Kate ran over to her Mama and Lena, "Roy is going to get the car to take me home. Come with us, Lena."

Lena shook her head, "I will not,"

"Please, Lena, please,"

"I will not." Lena said again,

Mama said, "Leroy's a nice boy. Now, Kate, you go right along with him. We'll see you at home."

Leroy came walking over to them, and he had the car keys in his hand. "Pop said they'll just walk on home. Come on, Kate."

The two teenagers climbed into the car. Even though Kate's house was in the opposite direction from where the Miller's lived, Leroy turned toward his own home, driving in front of the church and past his walking family. He drove close to his own home and then turned around and headed toward Troyers'. He went past his own walking family again, only this time he was meeting them, past the church again, and then on to Troyers'. He helped Kate out of the car and then he turned around again and headed home. He got home about the same time as the walkers.

The Millers were book readers and scholars. The Troyers were farmers. Mama and Papa saw no advantage for their children to go to high school. To farm, all you needed to know was how to figure out the cost of groceries and how much you would get for a crop, how many seeds you needed to buy for the land that was available, when to plant, what fertilizer to use and when to apply it to the plants.

Katie had Mr. Miller as a teacher and liked him a lot. There was no graduation ceremony when the children graduated from eighth grade. Their diplomas were mailed to them in the summer. None of the Troyer children went to high school. To go to high school in Limon, the family had to pay tuition. To go to high school in Mathison, it was a 16-mile trip. The Millers all went on to high school. At first Leroy caught a ride with a neighbor that took three other students and went back and forth to Mathison every day. Leroy's senior year, his brother, Frank, decided to rent a room in Limon and have Leroy live with him. Since they roomed in town they did not have to pay tuition. On May 24, 1926 Leroy graduated from Limon High school. He would be seventeen years old on June 24. He gave the salutatorian speech. He was the youngest person to graduate from Limon High School.

The family was quite proud of this oldest son, but being Mennonite they were careful not to show too much pride. Leroy enrolled in Hesston College in Hesston, Kansas for two years. This was a strict junior college. Lewis Miller's father, Noah, had donated the land and Lewis's sister Mary taught there. After two years, Leroy went to Greeley College. Roy called it, 'the best teacher's college in the state of Colorado.' So every September, Kate would watch her sweetheart catch the bus north. She would be nervous watching him go. What if he found someone else?

Chapter 15

Instead of going to high school, Kate and Lena had gone out to pick beans to earn money to help out the family. The first day had been a nightmare for Kate. It was a good thing that Lena had been with her so she didn't have to talk. She and Lena were hard workers and so, when Kate would just pick beans and not talk to anyone, that suited her boss just fine. She was quite the fast little bean-picker. The girls really didn't like the job, but every little bit helped. On the weekend, Papa came and took the girls back to the farm. On the weekends, Lena cleaned the house and Kate worked in the garden.

During the second year of bean picking, Lena got a job in the T.B. Sanitarium in La Junta. She liked it much better and the pay was better. That left Kate picking beans without her sister. She really missed her. After Lena had been at the hospital a-year-and-a-half there was an opening. She told her sister about it and soon Kate was working at the hospital, too. She cooked meals for the patients and then cleaned the kitchen after each meal.

Soon after Kate went to work at the hospital, Lena went to work for a wealthy man, taking care of his house. He paid her sixty dollars a month, which was a terrific raise from the twenty dollars a month she had been getting at the hospital. Kate continued working at the hospital for another year.

The money the girls earned was needed by the family. It was very difficult to make money on the farm. Mama did have some egg money but it did not stretch far enough to buy the sugar, coffee, salt, pepper, flour and other things not grown on the farm. Money was needed to buy gas for the car and coal to heat the house. Through their efforts on the farm and the girls' contributions, the Troyers lived comfortably. They did not go hungry because they had the meat they raised and the garden and the chickens and they always had at least one cow that they milked.

One weekend Kate said, "Papa, why can't we go to the wonderful new motion picture they are showing in Colorado Springs?"

Papa said, "What if the Lord would come and I was wasting my time reading or sitting in a theater watching a movie? He wouldn't go into the theater to get me."

Chapter 16

The year Kate was working at the hospital, they saved the hog butchering until Saturday. How she looked forward to that day. Of course, the butchering was bloody and everyone worked especially hard, but the visiting and seeing everyone made up for it. Her aunts and uncles all brought their equipment and each family brought a hog to be butchered. They had had the butchering at the farm when it was Grandpa's farm, so they still had it there. Everyone helped, so even though it was hard work, it was exciting.

Papa would get up at three o'clock on a cold, frosty morning and start a fire under the big, black fifty-gallon kettle used for dipping the pig so they could scrape off the hair. There was a smaller pot used to cook the hog's head and feet. About four o'clock the rest of the family would get up and begin fixing food and getting ready for company. It had to be a cold fall day so the meat would not spoil. Kate could feel the frost crunching under her feet and see her breath. Soon after that the other families would begin arriving.

They would bring the hog they were going to butcher in the back of their pickup or in a trailer if they drove a car. They would bring knives and any other equipment they had that could be used.

The men would slaughter the pig by shooting him in the head and hanging it head down from a trellis and bleeding it. Then, using a pulley, they dipped the whole pig up and down, up and down in the boiling water. Once again, using a pulley, they would move the pig to a table and then several people would help scrape off the hair.

The head and feet would be cut off and they would be put into a smaller pot and cooked so that the meat would fall away from the skull. This would be used to make head cheese. The feet would be pickled in vinegar. After the head and feet were done and taken out of the small pot, they would put the suet that had been cut into four inch cubes into the same kettle to render it and make it into the lard they would use for cooking and baking all winter long.

The entrails were washed and turned wrong side out and stuffed with spicy ground meat to make sausages for breakfast meals. The meat was cut up and made into slabs of roasts and chops and hams and bacon. The skin was left on the bacon and it was all dipped into a large kettle of water and the skin was scraped and scraped to remove any hair that had been missed. During the year, when they would finish eating a slab of bacon, the skin would be cut up and deep fried to make chitlings.

As soon as one hog was finished another was ready to be dipped and the process continued. Soon there were pigs at each step; dipping, scraping, making sausages or head cheese or lard or cutting the meat. Finally, all would be cut into slabs of meat for each family. Everyone worked but they also caught up on the gossip when there was a minute or two. Everyone helped with everyone else's hog. But no one worked harder than Sarah.

At noon they took turns eating the things brought by the different families. There was produce from the gardens, pies that had been made the day before, fresh pork from one of the pigs, and homemade bread. What a feast and what wonderful conversations. During lunch Sarah, Lena, Kate and Edna made sure that everyone was served, but that did not mean that they were left out. Everyone had their fill of food that day. There was always plenty of everything.

At the end of the day, the aunts and uncles and cousins climbed back into their vehicles. Instead of a live pig, they now had enough pork to last them until next year at the same time. Mama always said, "We use everything but the squeal." Mama loaded their pork into a big crock, packing it tight. It was buried in salty brine for a few days and then it was repacked and covered with salt for six weeks. Then the pig was put into the smoke house and smoked so that it would not spoil. It was kept there until they were ready to eat it.

They had a cellar that was away from the house that was quite deep. No matter how warm the days were the cellar stayed cool. This was where Mama kept the jars of vegetables and fruits she canned. In a way it was a wonderful place. But no one wanted to stay there long. It was also dark and damp.

When Mama canned she would use the same jars over each year, but the lids were usually new. It was foolish to risk losing food because of a poor seal. The food was picked, cleaned and cooked slightly. Then it was packed into jars and filled with boiling water. The jars were then put into a large kettle and cooked another 30 minutes. The boiling juices on the inside and outside would form a seal so that no air could get inside the jar and spoil the food. When a jar was opened, seldom would the food be spoiled.

Chapter 17

When Kate was seventeen her cousin, Obie Bontrager, came and lived with them. He went out and worked for other people but he slept and ate in their house. During haying season, he helped out on the farm. He and Papa were on a huge haystack. Their job was to form the hay so that the water would roll off when it rained. It was very important that the water not soak the hay. They stood on top and as other people threw up more hay, they would form the stack just right. While they were working Papa began telling Obie the way to Salvation. Obie stopped, stuck his fork into the hay, and said, "Say that again."

So Papa did.

Obie said, "I didn't know you just had to believe and have faith, and confess your sins, and ask Jesus to come into your heart. I thought I had to be twenty-one years old before God would even look at me." Obie accepted Jesus as his Savior.

Right after the haying season, Obie went home to his Amish relatives. He had to tell them the story of salvation. It was important that they be told that the promised Messiah of the Old Testament had come and He was Jesus.

That year Kate was still working in the hospital in La Junta. One of her co-workers came to her during the day and said, "When you get off work today, I'll be waiting by the back door of the hospital. I have something really important to tell you."

How the day dragged on. Kate couldn't imagine what was going on and she had all sorts of ideas running in her head. As soon as her shift was over, she went down to where her fellow worker was waiting.

"Kate," she said, "We have a chance to go to work at a home. There's enough work for both of us. Will you come with me?"

Kate had not thought of this. Change was hard for her. She liked working at the hospital and she knew what she was supposed to do. "I don't know. Maybe, I should just stay at the hospital."

"But, Kate," her friend argued, "we'll just be cooking and cleaning for one family instead of all those sick people and here's the clincher. . . " She paused for effect. "We'll be making ten more dollars a month." Kate did hate change but the added money sounded great and with a little more persuasion, the move was made.

It was soon obvious that her friend had known what a worker Kate was. At her new job, Kate became the cook and dish washer. Her friend was not a bit shy about giving Kate all the worst jobs to do.

After about a year, in the summer before her nineteenth birthday, Kate once more went home on the weekend. But this weekend was special. Roy was home from Kansas. He had been following a harvest during the summer and fall to help pay for the college classes he would start soon. He came to the house and had Kate go for a ride with him. He now had a car of his own. How Kate had worried that he would find a prettier and smarter girl at college, but here he was telling her about his plans to teach and asking her to marry him in two years.

When they were done talking, Roy walked her back to the door and Kate floated into the house, "Mama, Roy asked me to marry him."

Mama smiled. "I suspected as much. I'm not a bit surprised. Kate, you are going to have to start saving your money that you are earning. You will have your own home soon and you are going to need many things."

"But Mama, can you get along without my wages?"

"We always knew our sons and daughters would be leaving and having places of their own. Of course, we can."

"Oh, Mama, thank you. I am so happy."

Mama smiled. "Remember, Katherina, it's fun and good to be active. Enjoy your work no matter what it is."

Papa had been listening and he added, "Sometimes when you have something that needs to be done, you'll want to put it off. Don't, just go ahead and do it. It only gets harder as you put it off,"

Kate and Roy were both workers. She knew that most of the time it would not be too hard to follow the advice of her parents.

Chapter 18

It was about this time that Kate made another change. She went to work for Mr. Porter Thompson. He was a banker in Limon but he also had a farm. Since he didn't do the work, he hired six to eight men. How Kate dreaded the first day. She was so unsure of herself and had no idea what would be expected of her. She didn't know where anything was. She didn't know how much food to prepare and if there was a certain way to fix it. And she didn't want to draw attention to herself by asking questions. She worried about the men giving her a hard time. She worried about the Thompson children being mean. She worried about how she would get along with Mrs. Thompson.

Mrs. Thompson was much younger than Mr. Thompson. She had been quite a beauty when he married her. She was still very pretty. While he was at the bank, Mrs. Thompson would sit around. She did drink quite a lot of alcohol, Kate thought. But she was always pleasant and seemed pleased with the work that Kate did.

There were two girls and a boy in the family. They never had to do any work but they were nice to Kate. The oldest girl, Hannah, did like to think up things to do. It wasn't Kate's job to take care of them, but one time Hannah went swimming in the stock water that still had ice floating around on the top. A hired hand saw her and coaxed her out of the icy water and walked Hannah to the house. This time Kate did take over. She met them at the door and had Hannah go to her bedroom, take off her wet clothes and go to bed. For some reason this really amused Mrs. Thompson.

The younger sister, Teedie was very demure. She just went her own way, seldom getting into any kind of trouble. The little brother mostly just followed the girls around.

Kate's job was to fix three meals a day for the family and workers. She also cleaned the house. She did not do the laundry, which was a good thing. She was busy from daylight to dusk.

For the first time, Kate had a room of her own. The family slept in the second floor bedrooms. Kate had her own little room on the first floor. What a luxury. It was also a little lonely. But by the end of the day, Kate was usually ready to go to sleep.

On the weekends Kate would go home. She would always go to church with her family. She would visit with her brothers and sisters. She would help her Mama with her work, too.

Chapter 19

One Friday night Roy came over to the house when she was home for the weekend. Katie knew, by his grin, that he had something special up his sleeve. "Let's go for a walk." Kate ran and told her mom. Then off the two of them went. It was a beautiful evening. Kate loved the prairie. It was so open and endless. She waited for Roy to tell her whatever it was that had him so excited.

"Do you have any plans for tomorrow?"

Kate couldn't think of a thing.

"I've got big plans. You know who is coming tomorrow, don't you?"

Kate shook her head.

"It's an airplane, a real airplane. And it's not just coming here, it will give rides to anyone who pays. Can you imagine going up in the sky? Won't it be thrilling?"

"It would be," Kate said, "But do you know how much it costs? There is no way I can afford a ride."

Roy patted his pocket. "You don't have to afford it. I bought two tickets. Are you willing to go?"

Willing? Kate couldn't believe her ears. She had heard about the rides but knew she could not go, so she put them out of her head. "What are you going to wear?"

Roy thought a minute and then said, "Let's dress to the nines. Who knows when we will get an opportunity like this again. Agreed?"

Of course Kate agreed. It was like a dream come true. They went back to the house and told Mama. Roy said he had to head home and she walked him to the door. They agreed to go pretty early in the morning.

Kate got up with the sun. She did her chores. She couldn't believe it when she saw how early it was when she was done. She got dressed up in her church clothes and waited for Roy. She was very excited. Imagine going on an airplane ride in 1930. Some people had not even seen a plane, let alone ridden in one. Sure enough, Roy was eager, too. Here he came at least a half hour early. He was dressed in his very best clothes, as was Kate. He was driving his own car now so off they went. The plane was taking off and landing in a field about four miles from where Kate lived.

When they got there, they weren't the only ones coming for a ride. Some things were just worth the expense. There were a lot of looky-loos that had never seen a plane up close but couldn't or wouldn't go up in the plane. Most of the others were in their work clothes but Kate and Roy didn't care. At last it was their turn.

Kate climbed up on the wing and into the plane. She was sitting in front of Roy and behind the pilot. The pilot belted her in. There was only room for three people. The pilot took off across the field. It was such a bumpy ride. Then the plane left the ground and it was smooth, so smooth. Kate thought she might be a little frightened or nervous, but it wasn't so. It was so wonderful looking over the side of the plane. How the wind rushed into her face and through her hair. The people below looked like toys. The pilot tipped the plane sideways. Kate gasped, then she liked it. She was glad that she was belted in. The pilot would tip the plane one way and then the other. It was the most exciting thing she had ever done.

It was over too quickly. People had said that the rides were too expensive. Roy and Kate thought it was worth every cent. As they were driving home, Kate thought of all the wonderful times she had already had with Roy. She could hardly wait to begin her life as his wife.

Chapter 20

Whenever Kate had any time to spare, she would work on her wedding dress. It was the most beautiful white satin. It would have a rounded neck and long sleeves. It would reach below her knees, as did all her dresses. She also had sheer, white stockings and the most beautiful white satin shoes with high heels. To add to their glamour, they had white ribbons that tied across the top of her feet into the most enchanting bows.

On the day of the wedding, Kate put on her beautiful dress, stockings, and shoes. Her hair was perfectly done. In her hands she carried a large bouquet of white roses and baby breath with more white ribbons hanging down. She looked beautiful. She was shy. Roy was so bold and eager. He had on his black Sunday suit with a white tie. He also had a derby hat but he didn't wear it during the wedding.

Leroy and Kate were married August 14, 1931 in the Miller house with Reverend Lewis Miller presiding. The Mennonites do not wear rings so Roy gave Kate a wrist watch. They spent their wedding night in Manitou Springs. Then they camped out in the Rocky Mountains for a wonderful week.

Roy's first teaching job was a small school out on the prairie. He taught at Pattonsburg School District #18. It was a small school that was formed for the students that lived too far south of Hugo to be transported to that school. He was the only adult at the school. He had eighteen students from first through eighth grades. This was his second year at the school and he moved Kate into the small house that was provided for the teacher.

One of Roy's students was very slow and could not understand concepts very easily so he was also very disruptive. Since Kate had quit her job with Porter Thompson, when she got married, she decided to help Roy by working with Charlie a few hours a day.

The constant repetition, plus the fact that the student was dirty and not very respectful really got to Kate. But she hung in there since she knew that she was helping Roy and making his teaching job easier. She also fixed meals and cleaned the house and took care of the garden.

One Sunday morning, Roy and Kate left church. It was a lovely day, the sun was shining, and the prairie was arrayed in purples and yellows. Reverend Lewis Miller had preached the sermon and he always had you thinking about what he had said. He preached about a God that loved you, even if he disapproved of your actions.

Kate pointed in the direction of their house, "Look, it looks like a dust storm. Isn't that funny, the wind isn't blowing at all. Maybe it's a buggy or a car."

Roy took one look and stepped on the gas. Kate looked at him in surprise. His jaw was set. Kate turned toward the dust. Then she realized what Roy knew immediately. It wasn't dust. It was smoke. He drove at breakneck speed. When they got to the house, the fire was out but everything was still hot and smoking. Someone had carried her cedar chest, the china cabinet and stove in the yard. So those things were not burned, but everything else was gone.

"Our things, all our things." Kate said.

"It's all right." Roy said. "They're only things."

Kate was stunned. Their clothes, their food, the furniture she had bought with the money she had earned working for Porter Thompson, their books, everything was gone.

At first they just stood there looking at the smoke rising from what had been their house. As the property cooled they began looking around. They found a cast iron skillet that could be used again. They found dishes that were smoky but could be cleaned. They found a ham in the big crockery pot that was cooked to perfection. Kate said, "I couldn't eat a bite."

Lewis and Susie had a house that they rented out and it was empty at the time, so Kate and Roy moved into that house. It was farther for Roy to go to school but at least they had a place to live. Now Kate stayed home during the day instead of helping with the one student.

In April of Roy's second year he was called into the office of the school board president. He told Leroy that even though he was a good teacher, it was necessary for him to find another job. He was given the following letter:

> *Hugo, Colo.*
> *April 24, 1932*
> *To Whom it may concern.*
> *This is to certify that I personally know Mr. Leroy Miller as he has taught the Pattonsburg school for two*

> *years and has given good satisfaction. He is a young man of good habits and a fine Christian character and one that the pupils all like and I will cheerfully recommend him as a teacher to anyone.*
>
> *Respectfully,*
> *V. L. Aubert*
> *Treas. Dis't 18*

Leroy and Kate learned through the grapevine that the treasurer's nephew had just gotten his teaching degree and the family wanted his first job to be close to home. Roy immediately went job hunting. Since he was willing to take a job anywhere he could get one, he did find another small school in Bijou Basin. Again he was the only adult in the one room schoolhouse and he was responsible for teaching all eight grades.

Bijou Basin was a very small community in the high altitude of the Rocky Mountains. The school was very small. Each student was given individual studies. Kate and Roy lived in a small room that was attached to the school. There was no garden because the weather was too cold. There was no church in the community. Roy and Kate began to play chess. Kate quilted and read. She cooked three meals a day and soon after school started, she was feeling peaked. Then she realized that most food did not look at all appetizing in the mornings. Still, after she had been up a while each day she found she could function very well.

As the months wore on, she began to feel quite energetic and began sewing baby clothes. She made sure that she had eighteen diapers, as her Mom had told her that was how many she would need. She sewed shirts and made blankets for the coming baby. On March 11, 1933 Elizabeth Lee was born. It was funny how much more fun it was taking care of her own baby instead of a little brother. Her name seemed to be too much for such a little baby and soon everyone was calling her Betty or Betty Lee.

Now her days were full. Betty ate every four hours. Kate fixed breakfast and packed a lunch for Roy to take to school. He liked to eat with the students. Before he left for school, he would go outside and bring in a big pail of water from the pump. After Roy left, Kate would warm the water on the stove and fill a little tub and give Betty a bath. Then using the same water she would wash out the clothes Betty had worn the day before. Finally, she would wash the diapers. She would use a little wash board to make sure that everything was clean and then she would rinse everything and hang them outside on the line to dry. She cleaned the kitchen. She sang little ditties to Betty, such as 'Jesus Loves Me,' and 'Jesus Loves the Little Children,' and the 'B-I-B-L-E.' She told her stories from the Bible. Betty would nurse and sleep, and she loved to have Kate sing and tell her stories. Kate always had supper ready when Roy was ready for supper. After she did the dishes, she would sew little dresses and gowns for Betty. She started a quilt from all the scraps from the baby clothes. Roy graded papers and prepared for the next day. Sometimes they would play a game of chess after Betty went to sleep.

Chapter 21

In the summers, Roy would go to school at Greeley, Colorado to get his masters degree. He was adamant about getting it as soon as he could. He had a degree to teach all twelve grades but he majored in social studies and mathematics in the upper grades.

Kate and Betty went with him and in exchange for a room in Roy's uncle's house, she cleaned house and cooked for Uncle Sam and his wife. That way Roy did not have to work while he was going to summer school. This was the second summer that they had that arrangement. She knew that she was due that summer to have another baby, but she had survived morning sickness and both times had felt well in the later months. Kate's days were full but she also worked in the garden daily. That was not part of her duties but she enjoyed the time spent outside and she liked having the lettuce, radishes, squash, tomatoes and other fresh vegetables to prepare for meals.

When Betty Lee was fourteen months old, soon after they had moved to Greeley, Kate was working in the garden. She heard a loud pop and then there was the pain. She was so afraid that she had lost the baby. She went into the house and lay down on the bed. Betty Lee played on the floor beside the bed. After resting for an hour she struggled out of bed and fixed supper for Roy and the other family. The next few weeks were quite painful, but she did as much as she could and tried to ignore the pain.

Then it was time for her baby to be born, but nothing happened. Kate knew it was time by the constant movement and went to the doctor. He said, "She'll come when she's ready." Kate explained about the noise and pain for the past month. The doctor said, "When it's time for the baby to come, it will come." Kate knew things were not as they should be, but decided there was nothing she could do since no one listened to her complaints.

Then on June 20, 1934 there was a terrible pain. It was much worse than when Elizabeth was born. Apparently, some scar tissue had formed from the injury a month earlier. It was a good thing that her daughter was such a fighter. Helen Ann was born on June 20. She had forced an opening so that she could come out into the world. Kate's darling daughter, Helen Ann, would prove all her life to do what she set out to do regardless of the difficulty of the task.

So here she was with a brand new baby and Betty, an active toddler. Betty was too young to be any help and too old to be left unsupervised for even a moment. With Helen there were no relaxing nursings while holding the baby in her arms singing. If Mom did not keep one eye on her elder daughter and talk to her there was bound to be trouble. Helen had to be fed at least twice during the night.

The lack of sleep, chasing the toddler, cooking, cleaning and washing diapers kept Kate exhausted. She had worked hard all her life and was used to hard work.

That was a good thing. It had prepared her for motherhood.

After the summer was over Katherine and Leroy went back to Bijou Basin for his second year of teaching in that small school. Again there was no garden. Both Betty and Helen liked listening to stories and songs, so at a very early age Kate would tell them the Bible stories she had learned as a youngster. Some of them were: "Daniel in the Lions' Den" "Shadrach, Meshach, and Abednego and the Fiery Furnace," "Moses and the Burning Bush," " Joseph and his Coat of Many Colors" and many others.

At the end of his second year at Bijou Basin, it was decided that the school would be closed and the children bused to the nearest town. So once again, Roy went job hunting. He found a job in the small town of Korval. It was once again a one-room schoolhouse and Roy was the only adult. Even though he taught all the students, he was called the principal. This school was in the same district as the bigger school in Hugo, Colorado and they lived in a little house between the two towns.

Chapter 22

When Betty was almost three and Helen was a year and nine months old there was another addition coming into the family. The pains started and Roy didn't want to risk taking his family out into the blizzard. He went to his parents' house and called the doctor on the phone. The doctor lived in Limon but he told Roy he would get out there soon.

About three in the morning, there was no doctor but this baby was intent on seeing the world. The other births, Roy had made it a point to absent himself from the immediate vicinity. That wasn't an option this time. He was Kate's only help. So as the snow billowed and blew outside, Roy helped his third daughter make her debut into the world on the early morning of March 3, 1936. There was a touch of disappointment when he saw she wasn't a boy, but he was so happy that mother and daughter seemed okay, he tried not to let it show.

The sun came up and close behind it was the doctor. He took the baby from Kate's arms and told her to rest. He told Roy to take care of Betty and Helen while he rocked the baby.

Kate and Roy had picked out a name for a boy but none for a girl. So for the next few days they discussed different names. One day the discussion began with Roy saying, "I've got it. We'll name her Willamena and then we will call her Willie."

Kate thought about it for about a second. "If we're going to call her Willie, let's just name her Willie."

"Willie's not a name. It's more like a nickname." said Roy.

Kate laughed, "You're right. We need to think a little longer. I like the name Virginia."

Roy said, "You know, we have lots of Williams and Bills in the Miller family. How do you feel about naming her Billie?"

"Bill wasn't one of the names that we had decided on for a boy"

Roy said, "I really like the name Billie for this little girl." So Billie Virginia got her name.

Life was busier than ever. Betty thought she was an independent person. Betty also loved to play but she was a good little girl and was quite content with her place in life. Helen was a climber and would walk right off the edge of whatever piece of furniture she climbed on, so it was imperative that Kate rescue her before she reached the edge. Helen was always interested in what her mom was doing or any new activity taking place. She had an insatiable curiosity.

Kate remembered her own childhood years of taking care of Lyman and later Danny. She had a tender spot for her two younger brothers but she had determined that when she had babies, she herself would take care of those babies. This suited her oldest daughter to a tee. Helen, on the other hand, was quite interested in Billie. She would pat her and talk to her. She would rub her feet and often just play by her.

This summer, as in summers past, they went again to Greeley, Colorado. Kate's job was harder now since she had three little girls to take care of as well as the cooking and cleaning. Finally, in the summer of 1936 Roy got his master's degree.

After the summer sessions were over, they were headed home by the way of Lena's house. She had married Ora Davis and Kate was looking forward to spending a few days at her sister's house. After a few hours of driving, Roy asked Kate if she would mind taking the wheel. The girls were asleep in the back seat. Roy was leaning back and relaxing. Kate was driving the winding road of the Black Forest. Often there was a steep drop on the right hand side of the road. Kate didn't mind driving. She was taking her time and staying on her side of the road as she went around the curves.

Suddenly, a car came toward her. She was afraid to pull over, so she stopped. Her car was struck on the driver's door by a policeman. Kate would find out later that he was going after a poacher.

Kate was unconscious. The car still ran so Roy moved her over and drove into the next town to the hospital. After admitting Kate, he called his parents and Lena. Apparently, no one was hurt except Kate. She did not recover consciousness. Lewis and Susie took the three little girls and went on home. They told Roy that they would let Sarah and Daniel know about the accident and where the girls were.

Sarah came to the hospital. So Sarah, Roy and Lena took turns sitting with Kate. They would talk to her and sometimes they all sat in the room and talked. Kate did not respond in any way. On the third day they all decided to go have coffee. The two women felt they had to go back to their homes. They had men that relied on them. They assured Roy that they would help his folks with the girls.

While they were sitting in the coffee shop, a nurse came rushing into the restaurant to find Roy. Kate had awakened. She'd looked around and then said, "I have three little girls. Where are they?"

The nurse had told her that they were with their grandparents. Then she had gone to find Roy. Once Kate woke up, she was ready to leave the hospital. The next morning Roy and Kate took off for his parents' house. They spent two weeks there, as Kate was very weak and wanted to sleep a lot. Then the five of them went home.

Kate did the necessary things and let the other things go. Daily she regained a little more strength. She could hardly bear to let the girls out of her sight. She liked having them under her feet when she was working. Whenever one of them would move out of her line of vision, she would go and bring her back.

It was during the depression. Young people were going to school to become teachers and there were few jobs available. Again a relative of a school board member graduated and was given Roy's job. Once again Roy went job hunting.

He was once more given a letter of recommendation:

TO WHOM IT MAY CONCERN:

Mr. Leroy Miller has served as principal of our school (District 38, Lincoln Co., Colo.) for the past two years.

His instruction is thorough and his ability to secure the goodwill and cooperation of his pupils results in orderly and efficient accomplishment.

I sincerely recommend him for a position better than we can offer him.

Karval, Colorado
April 29, 1936

Geo. Ewing
secretary,

When the summer was over, Roy had a job in the Ellicott Consolidated School. Since it was a small school, he was given the job of principal and teacher. After school he coached the girls' basketball team and then the softball team. He would come home tired and still had papers to grade and lessons to plan.

Billie was very active and it was hard to keep track of her. After she was nine months old, Kate would put the dining room chairs on the table so she and Ann wouldn't get on the table and fall off. She'd lock the doors to the house while she did housework. Whenever Billie would go outside, she would always take off for long walks in a big hurry. It would seem that Kate would just deal with one of the other children for a minute and when she would look, Billie would be gone. The chase was on.

After losing her a few times, Kate knew she would have to watch her or hold on to her. After all, even if she didn't hurt herself, Kate had two toddlers that she could not leave alone to look for Billie. Once when Billie was just three years old, Kate found her walking on the railroad tracks. When Kate heard the train-whistle how she ran. Sure enough, there was Billie paying no heed to the whistle of the train. It was still a ways away but Kate grabbed her youngest daughter and carried her under her arm back to the yard. After this time, Kate always looked for her by the train tracks. Billie liked walking and sitting on the iron rails.

One day Kate went to the tracks, but no Billie. It had been raining and the ditch was full of water. How scared Kate was when she realized that Billie was lost. She started running toward the ditch. She met the dog on the way down so she knew she was headed in the right direction. Sure enough, there was Billie sitting on the edge of the ditch watching the water rush by. Again, the two of them hurried back to the yard where the older sisters were playing.

Billie also was always finding pets to bring home. Usually, they were little kittens and puppies that looked bedraggled. She would carry the latest acquisition around and give it lots of attention and care. She would lose interest when they no longer wanted to be cuddled and carried and loved. Kate was always giving away the healthy animals to make room for the needy ones that Billie would bring home.

Kate read a child's book to her three girls daily. Since she had few books for the girls she read the same books over and over. The children liked listening to the same stories again and again. Betty Lee and Billie were quite content to look at the pictures and listen to their mother read. Helen would squeeze right next to her mom so she could see the words.

A book salesman came by one day when Helen was still three years old. She was tiny and she was reading a book. The salesman said, "You'd think she was reading that book, the way she has it memorized."

Kate said, "She is reading it."

The salesman smiled and held up a book about the circus. "This is a brand new book that has just come out. If she can read it, I will give it to her." He handed the book to the tiny girl.

Helen looked at the book. She looked at some of the pictures. Then she turned to the first page of the story and read it perfectly. The salesman said, "If I hadn't seen it with my own eyes I wouldn't have believed it." He was as good as his word and he gave her the book.

Chapter 23

In 1937 the depression had hit Colorado and Roy was dismissed from his teaching job outside of Limon so the son-in-law of the school board member could have the job. So for the fourth time, Roy went job hunting. Jobs were hard to find. It was a disheartening loss. School teachers were not especially well paid but the money from this job did give the family a cash flow so they could buy the things not supplied by the garden and chickens and crops raised.

Then after a summer of stress and looking, Roy got a job in Morley, Colorado. There was no church in Morley, and Kate really missed going to church on Sundays. She had three children and sometimes she was lonely to be with other adults. Leroy was there in the evenings but he had papers to grade and lesson plans to prepare for the next day. Women were all busy during the day. They cooked from scratch. They sewed their own clothes. Many of them heated water on a wood-burning stove to cook and wash themselves, their dishes, their clothes and all other cleaning that needed hot water. The babies wore cloth diapers that needed to be washed. In the evenings when their husbands came home from their various jobs, the women waited on their husbands.

Then one day Kate was cleaning and Roy came home from school. She was so surprised. She thought it was only about 1:00 in the afternoon and here it was after 4:00. Kate scurried around and fixed supper and bathed the girls and put them to bed. They were usually in bed by 8:00 at the very latest. Kate would then quilt or sew clothes while Roy graded papers. Kate was a little flustered about the loss of the three hours but she just shrugged it off. She thought it must have been a result of whatever had caused her coma after the car accident.

The house they found was quite close to the school and by the summer of 1938 it was not unusual for the Miller girls to spend a little time at the playground daily. Billie had no fear of climbing the ladder of the slide but unless her mom was at the end of the slide to catch her, she refused to go down.

Sometimes the three girls would go to the playground by themselves. Morley was a small town and everyone knew everyone else. Kate could see the girls from a window as she worked and the girls knew that if they went anywhere else, they would lose the privilege of going by themselves. Then Billie would climb the steps of the slide and sit there for the rest of the time. After much coaxing by Helen and Betty for Billie to go down the slide, they would give up. Then they, and any other children playing, would just climb the steps and crowd past Billie to go down the slide. When it was time for the girls to go home, Kate would walk over and catch Billie at the bottom of the slide.

On February 12, 1940, Roy finally got his wish and Kate had a son. He was named Lynn Clifford, which made him L. C. Miller III. Roy's parents had moved to Manitou Springs, Colorado. Lewis was the preacher of the Mennonite Church. Since he was not paid for being a preacher, he also worked in a furniture store.

When Lynn was born, Lewis sent a letter to his son and daughter-in-law:

Dear Children,

So L.C. III finally arrived. Hearty Congratulations! I suppose Billie probably has thrown the cat out after Lynn came. We figured-Grandma and I- that the reason she kept the cat is to teach you all how to take care of Lynn Clifford after he came. Walk softly and whisper when he is asleep etc. etc.

Well sure enough that is fine. It tickled Grandma Miller so much that she laughed till she just about cried. She says no she didn't cry but she did not say that she wasn't tickled about it all. She and I concluded that after this year, Morley would be too small a place to Hold the distinguished Professor Miller and all His tribe of Millers - that is - at least not unless the City will give him a substantial raise in salary. To be real serious Girls are mighty nice but <u>it is fine to have a BOY</u> is it not? If you older folks are rather uncertain about that ask Betty, Helen, and Bill. Hope Helen is feeling fine again and that you will not get the measles now. That would be too bad. Have any of the other children had them.

Mother is feeling good today. Are looking for Doctor Stine over to look at the eyes. She sees a little more regular but still not distinctly at all. Doctor Nicks said he would judge that it will be about two weeks or more before she will begin to see good. She sits up to eat. That is propped up in bed with pillows, Still chokes some when she swallows. That is always hard on her. Makes her head hurt more. If we feed her real slowly she gets along better.

Some car salesman has been coming over here two or more times a day to trade cars with Jerry and me. He has a 37-V8 *sedan that he is offering us for $450 or -now- for our two cars and $200. If mother was well and we had no hospital bill or any other things to pay - I haven't - Jerry has - we might take a rap at him and get us a good car. But a good one would get a busted piston too, if it was run without water and oil just the same as a rattly one. So I guess we will let the 34 in the shed - especially since Jerry has his running good again.*

We had quite a bit of snow here too, but not like you folks. About half as much. We heard over the radio that there was more around Trinidad than in any other part of the state. (We wonder why they said Trinidad instead of Morley.)

Dons and Mary wrote that Idaho is really the place. While I was in Denver there were some FBI folks staying at the Hotel where I was. A man and his wife. They travel for the Government all the time. They said if they could do what they would like to do they would move out to Idaho and start an old Amish settlement out there–it wouldn't hardly do to join the Mormons! Do you folks want to go along when we go?

Well the youngsters are coming home from school and Bob will soon be here so I will draw this epistle to a close and get it ready for him to mail when he gets here.

We are very glad that Lynn Clifford made his arrival safely and that the fine Boy and his fine mother are both doing so fine. We know that the rest of the family are all fine too and we would surely like to run in and see you all. For the present however, we will have to stay on the job and see closely here. In a month or six weeks if mother keeps on improving, she will be able to walk around and go out to the table to eat with us again. That will surely be great. Yes, indeed it is great to be at home. We were both very much pleased when Dr. Jaeger came in and told us we could go home.

God bless you all. Write when you can and come to see us.

Lovingly the Dad

L.C.M.

Susie did go blind because of the brain tumor or the surgery and Lewis took care of her for the next twenty years. Susie learned to type during that time and wrote a book about her beloved Lewis in 1946 called *My Husband.* She also typed letters to her children that had left the area around Manitou Springs. She took up tatting and made doilies to go on the tops of dressers and tables. Lewis worked with her and encouraged and cared for her. They learned Braille together and he got her a New Testament in Braille. Sometimes at night Lewis would read aloud to Susie, but during the day she was on her own because he had to make a living.

Chapter 24

Sarah died of a blood clot on March 14, 1942. She had gone to the hospital because she felt so very ill. She seemed much better and had been released to go home. Suddenly, she collapsed on the floor as she was checking out of the hospital. They performed an autopsy to find the cause of her death. Daniel was devastated. Sarah had taken care of him for thirty-six years. She had carried much of the load for the past few years as Daniel had succumbed to asthma and sugar diabetes. She had cooked, sewed, mended and cleaned his clothes, cleaned the house, milked the cows, grown a garden, canned the summer food for the winter. She had given Daniel his insulin shots and been his comfort and companion.

Then Daniel had another blow. His two sons, Daniel and Lyman, that were still living at home, decided to join the army. Now Daniel was truly alone. He tried for a short time to take care of himself, but he knew it was not possible. Then he began living with one of his married children and then another.

On August 17, 1942, the last of the Miller children, Kathleen Rae, was born. How Kate loved that baby. She remembered the pleasure that her mother had derived from Danny and now she understood completely. She also remembered that her dad had been jealous of the attention that her mom had given to Danny, so she was careful to pay attention to Roy when he wanted attention, which was not very often. He was very busy.

One day Roy had come home with a new car he had bought for $900. It was so wonderful. The family decided to go pinon picking and off they went. The hills around Morley were quite fun to ride on. In the car Roy would sing with his children. He didn't sing the church songs that Kate would sing at night time. His songs were more roguish; "The Big Rock Candy Mountain" and "The Preacher and the Bear" were two of the songs he would sing. He also had sung "Little Brown Jug" while he had given his very small children rides on his foot that was up in the air when he crossed his leg. He also sang two other songs that never became popular. They were;

You Ask Me Why I'm a Hobo

You ask me why I'm a hobo
And why I sleep in a ditch
It's not because I'm lazy, no
I just don't want to be rich

———

Now I could make a million bucks
And eat 'til I got fat
But then I'd lose my girlish form
And, oh, I wouldn't like that.

———

Now I could be a banker

If only I wanted to be
But just the thought of an iron cage
Is too suggestive to me.

―――

Now I could eat out of dishes
It's just a matter of choice
When I eat out of old tin cans
There ain't no dishes to wash.

―――

Where the ――is they would all sing "doodlelydo, doodlelydo, doodleydo, do do

And
If You Want Your Girl To Love You

If you want your girl to love you,
If you want to be her beau
Then gather round and listen boys,
For you see I know.

―――

Put on your bib and tucker
And scrub your face real hard
Part your hair right in the middle boys
And slick it down with lard.

―――

Buy yourself some drugstore perfume

And sprinkle it on your clothes
A dimes worth will be a plenty boys
To tickle her little nose.

Tell her that you love her
And she'll become your wife
Or she will marry someone else
And hate you all your life.

What a wonderful day they had out in the woods. They had a signal. When it was time to assemble for lunch or to go home, Kate or Roy would yell, "You Hoo." If anyone heard the call they were to repeat it as loudly as they could and go back to the car. The day was cool as pinons are only picked after the frost has come. Fingers were black from picking the pinons out of the cones. But what a wonderful bunch of little nuts they had to eat when they got back home and Kate roasted them.

At the end of the day, they all climbed into the car and waited for Roy or Daddy, as the children called him. Kate couldn't imagine what he was doing. He seemed to be looking for something or someone. Kate got out of the car, "The children are all in the car."

Roy said, "I see that."

Kate waited, but when no more was said, she asked, "Is something wrong?"

Roy looked chagrined. "It seems I've lost the keys to the car."

Everyone got out and looked around the car but no keys. Roy had covered a large area, picking pinons and watching the four oldest children as they picked and played in the woods. At last they went back to the car. Kate and Kathleen got in and guided the car while the rest pushed it back on the road. Then they pushed it a little farther until they were on the top of a hill. Then everyone climbed in and they took off coasting down the hill and part way up the next hill. Just as they all piled out to start pushing again, a car came along and the driver offered to push the car to the top of the incline. So that was the way they got back to town. Another car would come along and push them to the top of a hill and then they would coast as far as they could and Roy and the three girls and Lynn would start pushing again up the hill. Nearly always a car would come by and they would be pushed to the top of the next hill. Finally, they were in town and a driver agreed to push him into the dealership so he could get another key.

The next day Kate roasted and salted the pinons in their shells. When the children played outside they would take some with them and eat them as snacks. It seemed like they ate and ate but were still hungry at suppertime.

Chapter 25

Kate had had several spells where she had lost two or three hours. She was quite perturbed by these spells but she kept them to herself. Everything was always all right when she would realize the time. Since she was nearly always at home she had never had a loss of time when she was out and about. The children were always fine so she just kept the worry to herself and didn't tell Roy about them.

It was impossible to get tires for the car as they wore out and finally the beautiful new car was sitting in the yard unable to go because the tires had worn out. Times got harder and money got tighter and one day Roy came home and said he had sold the car. Kate was quite sad but she knew Roy was too, so she said, "It's just as well. It was just sitting there. We had no tires or gas."

In 1941, Helen Ann had lots of pain in her legs. The doctor told Kate and Roy that she had rheumatism and the best thing they could do for her was to move to a hot, dry climate. Roy applied to places in the desert of Arizona. Then one day a letter came. There was an opening in mathematics in the high school of Casa Grande for the 1942-1943 school year.

Now another car was needed. Of course, the one Roy bought was not nearly as good as the one he had so recently sold, but it did have tires. Billie started first grade in Casa Grande. The three girls had played school so much that the first grade teacher called Kate in and told her, "Billie could go into second grade and not have any trouble. The only problem she has is she makes her cursive capital 'I' backwards. If she could correct that she should fit right in with the other second graders."

How Billie practiced that night, though she couldn't see the point. Her capital 'I' looked the same as the teacher's. The only difference was where they started when they would make them. But Billie thought it would be nice to move to second grade so she practiced the capital 'I' the way the teacher had shown her. Helen Ann and Betty had both skipped first grade. The difference was that they stayed in the same room, since they were in a one-room schoolhouse. Billie had to move into a room with children that she did not know that were all a little older than she was,

One day Billie was going to go to a friend's house after school. She had given her mother directions for the way to go to pick her up. "Go down our street until you come to the house with lots of clothes on the line. Then you turn by that yard and go to the corner house that had a yellow car. Finally, you turn there and I will be at the house with a red wagon in the front yard."

Kate said, "I'll be there at 5:00. Be ready to come at that time.'

During the day Kate suddenly realized that every direction Billie had given her was based on objects that could be moved very easily. What if the woman took in the clothes, what if someone took the car for a drive, what if the wagon was in the back yard and she could not see it? She did her household chores and worried.

Maybe she should pick up Billie at school after all. No, that would not do. Billie had been so happy about this extra responsibility. She knew the girl's name. She would be able to find her if it became necessary.

Five o'clock rolled around. Kate told Roy, "I'm going to go get Billie. I'll be right back." Under her breath she added, "I hope."

She drove down the street. There were the clothes on the line. She turned and went until she saw a yellow car at the corner. She turned and came to a house with a red wagon in the front yard. She pulled up in front of the house. She was just thinking of going to knock on the door when out came Billie. She was happy to see her mom, but she was also excited about her visit and talked about the fun she had had all the way home.

One Saturday Kate went to the grocery store in Casa Grande. The children were all at home with Roy. Kate realized that she had no idea where she was. The clerk was saying, "Please, that will be seven dollars and twenty-six cents." Kate had her purse in her hand so she dug out some money and gave it to the clerk. She started to walk off without her groceries and the clerk yelled at her, "Here, don't forget your sack." She heard the clerk and person behind her in line laugh at her, but she just took the bag and walked outside.

Where was she? How did she get here? "Don't get scared, don't get scared," she told herself over and over. In her head she saw a car. She walked right out to the parking lot but there was no car like that. Then she saw it. It was across the lot. She went out and climbed into the car. Now what? Where should she go? "Don't get scared." The refrain kept going on inside her head.

She found her car key and stuck it into the car. It fit. She started the engine and she knew. She knew. She drove home. That was the end of her blackouts. Whenever one threatened, she could talk herself out of it.

Betty, Helen, and Billie were gone all day to school. Kate was home with Kathleen and Lynn. How the two children would argue and fuss at each other, but then they would go through long periods of time when they entertained each other and would laugh and play together. If anyone intervened in their arguments, the two would immediately join forces to tell the would-be mediator to 'mind your own business.'

Chapter 26

In 1944, the family moved to the mountain town of Flagstaff. The opportunity came up in January. If Leroy wanted the position he had to take it right then. So he did. He moved to Flagstaff and began work the first day in February. He moved into a tiny apartment. He went out most nights to play cards or take a college class and to spend time with unmarried men in town. Kate had stayed back to sell their house in Casa Grande and to let the children finish out the school year.

Roy was looking for a place big enough for the family. Housing was at a premium. The Navajo Ordinance Depot had opened in 1942. It needed many workers. As people came to work at Belmont, many lived in Flagstaff and made the trip back and forth. Many people gouged renters by charging exorbitant fees for very small places.

"*War Housing Project No. 2221 was located northwest of Antelope Spring and today's Flagstaff Middle School. The project was named Clark Homes in honor of pioneer John Clark, who formerly ranched on the site. Clark Homes, as a federal project, was first occupied by ordinance and other war workers along with army and navy personnel. With two hundred units and hundreds of children, it soon became a village unto itself.*

Eventually, everyone from college administrators and professors to depot laborers lived in Clark Homes. For some it became 'the place to live' in town and they couldn't wait to move in. For others 'it was a pit.' The homes resembled military barracks with thin walls that did little to keep noises out or warmth in. Fumes from kerosene used in heating and cooking were especially unpleasant." (Westerlund, John S, *Arizona War Town* page 191).

Roy had been hired as a mathematics teacher but he was also given the job as the assistant football coach at Arizona State College (ASC) of Flagstaff. He had wanted to go into the service but no way would they consider taking a father of five children. In Flagstaff he felt like he would be helping the war effort. The Navy had a V-12 program and he was to teach algebra, analytical geometry, and calculus as well as swimming and wrestling and judo to the navy men that were then stationed in Flagstaff. He studied the wrestling and judo holds carefully, and Roy thought he was quite capable of teaching them. The swimming was another matter. He always felt inadequate as a swimming instructor. He had had little experience swimming and had never learned to dive. While teaching, he would watch for a very capable student to show off and then had him demonstrate the movements.

He was a very capable higher mathematics teacher. Perhaps before the navy moved in, some of the more complex subjects were not taught as well as they should have been. "*After the navy landed, however, 'that all changed' because the navy demanded top-level instruction. The college curricula improved and the faculty relished the opportunity to expand the depth and scope of their instruction.*" (Westerlund, page 220)

When school was out in Casa Grande and the house was sold, Kate and the children moved to Flagstaff. Because Roy was working at ASC with the navy, he had been able to rent a three-bedroom home in Clark Homes. There were no formal yards. But the area around the houses was tall ponderosa pine trees and native bushes. A garden was not feasible in Flagstaff, because there were just a couple of months a year when the weather did not freeze. It was less than 200 miles from Phoenix but the altitude was almost 7000 feet. The walls of the houses were thin and much of the time the house was cold.

Though it was disappointing not having a garden, for the first time in her married life, Kate had leisure time. She began quilting more. She had a lot of scraps since she made shirts for Lynn and dresses for the girls. The Millers played bridge on a regular basis with the Derifields. Kenneth Derifield taught at the college like Roy, and his family also lived in Clark Homes.

The children in the neighborhoods played well together. One summer the yards that had no grass, only pine needles and rocks, had little houses appearing everywhere, There were board houses, stick houses, rock and mud houses. Some of the children even tried to make a house of mud and pine needles. Since the houses were about four feet square, the fun was in making them not being in them.

The Millers joined the Baptist Church that was on the corner of South Beaver Street and Cottage Avenue. Once again, Kate became a Sunday school teacher. It wasn't what she wanted but she did feel that was where the Lord wanted her to be. Again, she knew the young children but did not really become well acquainted with the adults.

Chapter 27

Betty, Helen, and Billie were going to the training school on the campus of the college. Arizona State College in Flagstaff had been a teacher's college before the war. Billie was in fourth grade and her teacher was Miss Kell. Billie loved her as a teacher. She told wonderful stories. One day she took her class on a walking field trip to Lowell Observatory. Each child was allowed to look through the giant telescope. Lo and behold, you really could see stars in the daytime. They had learned that the sun was the closest star but on that day they could see other tiny lights in the sky. After that, they walked down the hill, ate a picnic lunch in the park, played on the equipment, and then walked back to school.

On Sundays the family would go to church and then go eat lunch at the faculty dining room. The family had never had the money to eat out so Kate thought this was quite wonderful. It was one very nice meal a week when someone waited on her for a change. Unfortunately, when the summer was over, the Millers were told that they could continue to come but they had to leave the children at home because of the limited space. That was the end of the eating out. The Millers didn't leave their children with others.

Once in a while, Roy would be able to take the family swimming in the college pool. It was fun to be the only ones there. Roy would practice his swimming by working on the strokes that his students had learned during the week. All the children learned to swim that year. Betty became an excellent swimmer. Lynn was an endurance swimmer. He was not very fast but he could swim forever, it seemed, without getting tired.

While living in Flagstaff, Betty Lee decided everyone was to call her Elizabeth and Helen announced that she preferred her middle name Ann. The family was quite accommodating and, when they remembered, they made the change.

As Lynn's teeth came in, they were chalky and there were many trips to the dentist. Roy and Kate were very concerned. Fortunately, as his permanent teeth came in they were better.

The winter was cold but not awful. The sun shone many days in the winter. The children enjoyed playing in the snow and the young house builders tried building an igloo in the front yard. They finally had to put boards across the top and pile snow on the boards because without the board the roof kept falling in. From the outside it looked quite authentic to the children.

Elizabeth occasionally would babysit and with some of her money she bought a pair of ice skates. Near Clark Homes was a pond where the water ran when the snow melted and it froze enough to skate on in the coldest days. If Betty was skating, of course, she would wear the skates. But if she was busy, she would loan them to Ann or Billie. It was so much fun to go skating across the pond. Many other children were there after school and on Saturdays and life was good. Once Roy tied their sled to the bumper of his car with a stout rope and gave them exciting rides on the frozen snow. There was also a hill close to the observatory where the traffic was closed off so the children could go down the hill. They couldn't afford a store-bought sled, so Roy made them one out of wood. Actually, the other children found it quite fascinating because you had to turn it with the weight of your body. It was quite a challenge, if you didn't get a straight start.

One of the highlights of living in Flagstaff was the all-Indian powwow over the Fourth of July weekend. As much as a week before the actual powwow, Indians would begin coming into the city park that was within a block of Clark Homes. Families would come in their wagons pulled by horses. If they came through Cameron, Arizona the person running that trading post would have an orange for each person. As they entered the northern part of Flagstaff, the Greers had a trading post and restaurant on highway 89. They would give each family a watermelon. Jimmie Lee Greer said, "The first Indian powwow each year is across the street from our buildings."

Roy traded with the Indians. He got Kate a silver bracelet and earrings and a ring set. She wore the bracelet the rest of her life. He also traded a reversible shiny coaches' jacket for a petrified wood ring and bracelet. There was a fee to get into the Indian dances and rodeo so the Millers didn't go to those. But they could walk through the booths and talk to the families and see the wonderful turquoise, silver and other jewelry. They had rugs made from the sheep they had raised. Roy insisted and bought one for Kate. She put it on the floor by their bed. It was nice. It had red, black and gray, and white colors. It was wool and it was warm.

One night Kate and the children were standing watching the free demonstrations of Indian dances. They were not very long and were used to entice people in to watch the dancing. One young male dancer was twirling and dancing. He was quite acrobatic and when he raised his leg very high, Kate saw that he had nothing on under his buckskin. She twirled the children around and immediately took them back home.

Chapter 28

Roy had coached before, but it had always been an extra job after school for extra money. He found he was not fond of it. He would put in long days as he coached after teaching other classes. Coaching was hard on Roy. If the team did well, the team was lauded. If the team lost, the coaches were at fault. Besides, he did not feel that he was more than adequate as a swimming instructor. Also, Ann had been freezing ever since moving to Flagstaff. Her teacher called Kate and told her that she needed to dress Ann more warmly as she shivered all day long at school. Kate explained to the teacher that since Ann was in sixth grade she could dress as she pleased as long as she was dressed modestly. Kate did go to Ann and talk to her about dressing more warmly, but Ann said that she was getting along just fine. Roy and Kate talked about everything and decided once again to move back to the warm desert. So once again he started looking for another job. He was offered a job by the Yuma High School Board and was told that they had a 'lovely home' for them to live in if he took the job. The lovely home was much like their home in Clark Homes only it was a remodeled Army barracks eight miles from Yuma on an Army base.

    Now the children and Roy all made the long ride to school every day. Sometimes they would go with Roy but since he stayed longer than they did and it was already a long day, they would ride the school bus home. Kate took Kathleen and went house hunting. Soon the family moved into a three bedroom house in a quiet neighborhood in town.

It was during this time that Elizabeth took up the clarinet. There was a big tree out in front of the house. Occasionally, she would climb up into the tree to practice. Everyone around either ignored or enjoyed the noise except for one neighbor lady who would complain and complain.

Billie, Lynn, and Kathleen would spend many hours acting out the movie they had seen the previous weekend. Often they would take turns being Roy Rogers or Gene Autry or even Bob Nolan, the lead singer of the Sons of the Pioneers. They would spend the day running and hiding and shooting the criminal of the day with their pointed fingers. Ann didn't usually play because she was reading.

Lynn should have started school in Flagstaff but he was diagnosed as having undulant fever. He was quite sickly. He also had a heart murmur. He was to stay in bed. This was almost an impossible task. He took after the Troyer side of the family and thought he should always be doing something. Roy and Kate and his big sisters had taught him at home, so he wouldn't get behind. He was quite sure this was not how life was supposed to be. His joints hurt and he did have some stomach trouble but this staying in bed was not for him. Ann, Elizabeth, and Billie had all skipped first grade because of the learning they had received at home. Lynn was different than the girls. He could tell you any answer just as quickly as they could, but when he was to write an answer it was another story. How he hated writing.

When the V-12 program was nearly over and the Millers had moved to Yuma, Roy's good friend, Kermit Dale had moved to Mesa to teach algebra, geometry, trigonometry and calculus at Mesa High School. After a few years Kermit decided to move to California. He wrote to Roy and told him that his position in Mesa would soon be available. Roy and Kate talked it over. The girls were growing up. Tempe had a very reputable college. If they moved to Mesa, the girls and, later, Lynn and Kathleen could live at home while they got a college degree. He applied for and got the job. He went ahead of the family and bought a three bedroom home. Then he went back and got the family. Once again, Kate could have a garden. There was a lovely lawn in front and a garden and a cow in the back that Kate or Roy would milk twice a day. They got a small black cocker spaniel and called him His Nibs because he got so much attention.

It was a small house. The girls shared a bedroom with two double beds that almost filled the room. There was a dresser between the beds and very little floor space. When the girls lay in bed in the dark at night, they would play many different games together. Sometimes, they would play memory games, often based on the alphabet. Other times, they would say states, cars, movie stars, singers on the radio, dogs, or trees; there were endless lists. In another game, one of the sisters would say a state and another sister had to say the capitol. Sometimes one would say a word and the next would need to say a word that started the way that word ended. Billie learned her multiplication tables in bed at nights and memorized the names of the books of the Bible. She memorized the presidents' names and the capitols of the states. Sometimes they would play rhyming words with Kathleen. Sometimes Ann would not play because she would be reading a book under the covers by flashlight.

The same games were played when they were doing the dishes. They would also sing songs with the radio. One would wash dishes, one would dry and one would clean off the table and sweep the dining room. The chores would change at the beginning of each week. Billie enjoyed the camaraderie. Elizabeth thought it all boring. Ann seemed content no matter what was going on. She was always interested in her surroundings. Though she often had her head in a book she usually knew what was going on.

Sometimes on weekends they would play hide-and-seek inside the house. Billie found out that if she hid in the wide bathroom closet with a little door and left the door open, the person who was it would glance into the closet and would not see her hiding in the clothes, and then they would close the door. She was often accused of going outside, against the rules, when she would come running in and shout 'free.'

One day, Roy bought the family an Indian pony. The children would have to work hard to get him to go away from home. If the rider would relax for a minute he would turn around and head home. Often they would have to kick him with their heels to keep him moving away from home. Ah, but when they turned around and headed home, they would have to hold on, because off he would go at his fastest gallop. The ride home was always exciting. Because of his black coat with a star on his nose, he was named Midnight.

One day little Kathleen was on the pony behind her brother, Lynn. They were in the field next to the house. They had only gone a very little distance from home, so they were so surprised when Midnight lifted his head and started for the backyard at a hard run. Kate started running after him shouting, "The clothesline! The clothesline! Kathleen, Lynn, lean down, lean down as far as you can. He's running right for the clothesline!" Midnight ran around the house and into the backyard. Kate could clearly envision that line hitting her children in the neck. She was running as hard as she could, cutting across the field. Midnight ran straight toward the clothesline. Lynn was struggling to get his arms loose so he could haul back on the reins but Kathleen had wrapped her arms around his in a panic and wouldn't let go. At the last second, Midnight stopped. A screaming Kathleen stayed on until Kate had climbed the fence and pried her loose from her brother and lifted her down. While the mother and daughter had been terrified, Lynn had the ride of his life. Kate said a reverent, "Thank you, God," and took Kathleen into the house. Roy unsaddled the pony and turned him loose in the backyard.

Kate and Roy were especially nice to Lynn and Kathleen that night. They were so happy that they were not hurt. "You'd think we were heroes or something." Lynn said with a grin.

Chapter 29

The family was very engaged in church activities. They went to church for two hours on Sunday morning and one hour on Sunday night. Lunch was often at Rendezvous Park after church. A lovely afternoon was spent reading and playing ball, and the children sometimes went swimming. The children went to a youth meeting on Tuesday nights, and everyone except Roy went to prayer meeting on Wednesday evenings. Ann, Elizabeth, and Billie went to choir practice on Thursday nights.

On Wednesday nights Roy went to the Elks Club and played in a big money poker game. He didn't have the finances but he was good enough that he had a backer that would put up the big bucks and give Roy a percentage if he won and just take the few losses.

Kate would read a short passage from the Bible at the breakfast table before the blessing. In the mornings usually everyone in the family was present. Often for supper one or more of the family members was missing. Elizabeth and Ann would often babysit and Roy might have meetings that would make him late.

Roy shot the gun that started each high school game and kept time during the games. He would sit down close to the team next to the field. Kate would take the children to the games. They would sit in the stands and cheer for the home team. Between church and school activities the family was busy and happy. Kate sometimes thought it would be nice to be around other adults. Occasionally, all or some of the family would play board games. Often, Ann and Kate would take on Elizabeth and Roy in bridge. They had a ping pong table in the back yard that became warped with the weather. Because of this the players never knew which way the ball would bounce and they all got quite good at ping pong.

Elizabeth, Ann, and Billie all took piano lessons. They each had to practice for 30 minutes each day, so for an-hour-and-a-half a day the piano was being played. It was a chore to practice, but they all wanted lessons so practice they did since that was the condition if they wanted lessons.

Then they had a chance to move. They could rent ten acres from Mr. Palmer. The land had a house with a huge living room, a big enough dining room, a large bedroom upstairs and two bathrooms. Downstairs it had a basement with a very large bedroom, a small bedroom, and a pantry in the hallway at the end of the stairs between the two rooms. Once again the girls shared the huge room downstairs. It was the most room that they had ever had and all four girls were quite delighted with it. Finally, each girl had an area that was her very own. Lynn had the small room.

The basement was always cooler than the rest of the house. In the summer, it was very comfortable sleeping there. In the winter, the children wore warm pajamas or nightgowns and had plenty of blankets on their beds. Some of their sheets were made of flour sacks. When they made the beds after doing the laundry on Saturdays they would make sure that the seams were up on the bottom sheet and down on the cover sheet. They also made all their dishtowels out of flour sacks. Sometimes in the evenings they would sit around and embroider pictures on them.

The house also had a huge screened-in porch with a sink. It was a luxury that they had never had before. Because they weren't used to it, they would mostly spend evenings outside rather than on the porch unless the mosquitoes were out. Next to the porch was a rather small room that was used for storage.

Now there was enough room so Kate could help take care of her dad. The small storage room was cleaned out and they put in a chest of drawers and a twin-sized bed. It also had a small closet. In the winter it became Grandpa Troyer's room. The summers were too hot for him so each year Kate and Roy and usually Kathleen and Lynn would take him back to Colorado to Lena's house. For the last years of his life, he would spend six months at each daughter's house. When he was in Colorado, Elizabeth would move into his room. The house had no refrigeration and this room only had a fan.

Kate said, "Isn't it awfully hot?"

Elizabeth said, "I don't care. I want a room all my own."

For Kate, the land was the most exciting part. There were seven-and-a-half acres of pasture. Out in one pasture were half-a-dozen peach trees. But the-two-and-a-half acres that the house was built on were the most exciting for Kate. There were date trees, a lemon tree, grapefruit trees, naval orange trees, pecan trees, an English walnut tree, and even a kumquat bush.

Not too far from the house was a chicken coop. It had a place for nesting inside and a fenced area for chickens to run around in the daytime. There was a huge area where they could park their cars. It wasn't paved but the dirt had been packed firmly down. There was a huge building made out of laths with small spaces between each lath. Soon Kate had a garden in the front yard, and rabbit pens were put into the lath house. In the summer Kate would spray the pens with the hose several times on the days when the weather was over 100 degrees.

They put their cow in one of the pastures and they got a pig. It wouldn't stay in the pen. So about once a week the family would go out and herd it back and Roy would fix the fence where he got out. Sometimes there were holes in the fence. Sometimes there were holes under the fence. They just didn't look big enough for the pig to get out, but he did get out over and over again. Then one morning he was out but there was no hole. Roy had systematically tried to cut off every escape route. Now he could simply not see how the pig had gotten out. The family herded him back into the pen. Sure enough, the next morning he was out again.

Roy said, "One of you children must have let him out."

There was a chorus of, "I didn't."

Everyone was told to keep an eye on the pig to see how he kept getting out. After he was put back for the fifth time, with no hole in sight, Kate had had enough. She took a book and put a reclining outdoor chair where she could see the pig pen. She would read while keeping an eye on the pig. She kept glancing toward the pig. She couldn't believe her eyes. The pig was climbing the fence. It was wire but who would have thought it! The pig was right at the top, when she went and pushed him back into the pen. Then she went to tell Roy. They would now need to put wire across the top, too. What a nuisance! They decided that was what they would do the following weekend.

At school the next day, Roy was complaining about his run-away pig. He only ran from his pen into the field with the cow. A teacher that had pigs said, "What you need is to get him a companion. Pigs hate to be alone."

So that weekend, Roy and Kate went and got a young pig and put them together. It was amazing; the pig did not run away again. From then on, when the bigger pig was butchered, they would replace him with a young pig.

Roy soon bought several cows to milk morning and evening. He sold the extra milk to Roosevelt Dairy. The pig wasn't the only animal that would get out. Midnight had a place to run but he had to be kept separate from the cows. Otherwise, he would chase them around the field and they would not give as much milk. The field was in three two-and-a-half acre lots. The cows would be rotated so alfalfa would have a chance to grow for a while before they would graze. Midnight was always kept in a different field than the cows. He would eat such a little bit that his presence made no difference. He much preferred grain to alfalfa anyway. But he did love to get out. Sometimes he would get in with the cows. Sometimes he would head down the road. He would go about five miles away to another farm in Lehi. When Grandpa Troyer was there, he would get in the car and go get him. Midnight always came to him as Grandpa would always have some grain. Grandpa would put a bridle on him and tie him to the back of the car and drive slowly home.

When someone was riding on Midnight's back he would still fight going away from home. Palmers had a cattle guard that went into the property. When leaving, he refused to go over the cattle guard that the cars drove over. Going away from home he would go down into the irrigation ditch, which was usually dry, and up the other side. Returning at a dead run, he would jump over the cattle guard and be home. No one in the family really knew how to sit a horse so he did pretty much as he wanted. They all agreed that going like the wind on the way home was fun.

One morning he was lying on his side. He had been tied in the yard and he got tangled up with the rope. Ann noticed it first and went out to let him loose. The rope had really cut into his leg above his foot and it was a nasty rope burn. Because of his injury, he couldn't be ridden. Roy would clean the wound twice a day and put medicine on it. When he was healed, Roy sold him to the man he kept running to in Lehi since the children were busy with other things and no longer seemed interested in riding a horse.

Chapter 30

One cow had come with them from their previous home but now there was lots of room, so Roy slowly began to get more and more cows. He made a deal with Roosevelt Dairy to put creamers out at the end of the driveway every morning for the company to take and sell. At first he milked the cows outside in a pen. The cows would come in to the pen to be milked. When they put their heads into the stanchion to eat the oats, Roy would fasten them in until he was done. The shed had a very leaky roof and there was space between the slats of wood so that the air could circulate. Rain and then mud was really a mess but that was not near the problem that the heat was. When he had a few cows, the outside shed was fine, but it didn't work as well once he had acquired more cows.

Because the town was growing, Roosevelt Dairy said the only way they could continue to use the Millers' milk was if the family put in more modern equipment and a milking barn. Roy measured the floor the following weekend and put two-by-fours around the outside edge. He also put boards down the middle of the floor. Then he had a man with a cement truck come and pour cement into the two sections of floor. Then the work began. There were two-by-fours that reached across the floor. Then a family member sat at each end of the pieces of wood. Working with the person at the other end, the boards were used to pound the air out of the cement to make it level. How the family pounded! Up and down, up and down went the pieces of wood. After awhile, each child put his or her handprint into the cement. Roy wrote the date that the floor was put in.

The following weekend the milking barn was built. What a wonder! It had two rooms. The walls were block. The whole family worked on it. It was hard work carrying mortar and blocks and putting the milking building up one block at a time. Maybe the walls weren't perfectly straight but they did the job. One room was for milking. The other room had a large stainless steel refrigerator and a series of bars that were very cool. The cream can was under the bars so that by the time the milk was in the cream can it was cold.

The work took place in the other room. Roy splurged and bought a milking machine. Two cows were in the milking barn at a time. They walked up a sloped cement surface into the barn and then would go into the stanchions. Roy always had oats in the feeder of the stanchion so the cows would come in and start eating the treat. If the first stanchion had a cow, the next cow would pass her and go into the leading stall. The barn was just the right size so that the cows stood one in front of the other to be milked. As soon as one cow came in, Roy or Lynn would wash the cow's udder and check for mastitis. If the milk from each teat was flowing, Roy would put the milking machine on the cow. Then father or son would wash the other cow and get her ready for the machine.

During the milking, there would be a short break while the milking machine worked and the males talked about their respective days. Roy would help Lynn study for up-coming tests and give him advice as he felt the need. When the milking machine was done, one of them would strip the cow by hand and the other would walk up the four steps to a platform and pour the milk into a container with a strainer. The milk would flow through a tube into the next room and over the cooling coils and into a cream can.

Lynn would release that cow and fasten the next one in. There was an 'in' door and an 'out' door so the cows never turned around inside the milking barn. Most cows were eager to be milked and there would be a line waiting for their turn. There were usually one or two cows that did not get into the line or got tired of waiting and would go back out into the field. As they got down to the last cow in line, Lynn would send his German shepherd dog, Scaramouch, out into the field. Did he get the same cow each day? Did he nip all the cows' heels until one of them came to be milked? Lynn was never sure of the reason, but here came his dog with the missing cow or cows.

Chapter 31

Lynn was such a help in the yard and with the animals, Roy decided to give him his own heifer. He raised that girl on a bottle and it followed him everywhere. She was his pet and he could do no wrong. Lynn got it into his head that if he lifted her up every day, one day he would be lifting a cow. He would be the strongest man in the world. So every morning he would go out and carry his calf around. Soon he was just lifting her for a few minutes and putting her back down. Then one day it happened. He simply couldn't get all of her up in the air at one time. It wasn't her weight as much as her size. She was just too big to handle. She still loved him and would come at his call.

Then she had a calf of her own. Suddenly, she would have nothing to do with Lynn. She would run at him if he tried to get near her calf. One day, he was on the stack of bales of hay. No matter which side he tried to climb down, she would charge him and chase him back up. Roy finally saw what was going on and went and chased the cow away.

After the calf was weaned, she once again liked Lynn. Then one day she got in with the bull and had her leg broken. Roy and Kate and Lynn put a splint on it and bandaged it up. Every morning they would go out and stand up the cow. Every evening they would go out and lay her back down. People laughed at them and said, "You butcher and eat a cow with a broken leg." But they said, "Not this cow you don't." She did get well and she also gave very rich milk.

Later on, they decided to get a lamb and raise it to butcher for mutton. They were able to get a black lamb for a very cheap price. They named him Danny. He was so cute and tiny! The children took turns feeding him with a huge bottle. It seemed that he just could not learn to eat without the bottle. He should have been weaned but when he was left with food or water he wouldn't touch it. He'd just bleat and bleat. So three or four times a day he would be bottle fed.

Then one day Kate saw him running over and drinking from the cows' water. Sure enough, he showed no interest in the water in his pen and greedily grabbed the bottle with his teeth and sucked. Kate said, "If he can drink the cows' water he can eat and drink like all the other animals." She put his food and water in pans and went off and left them. How Danny bleated for his bottle! He sniffed his food and bleated some more. Kate went into the house and watched him through a window. After several minutes, Danny went over and ate his food and then drank water from the bowl. He was never bottle fed again.

Elizabeth occasionally went out on dates with some of the boys from church. One of the boys was Robert. He was very correct. He always would pick her up at the door and open the car door for her and hold her arm like she was fragile. Billie and Kathleen thought he was too stuffy for words. Danny didn't bother many people but he sure didn't like Robert. How he would try to butt him! Robert figured out that he would not butt Elizabeth, so when he walked her to the car he maneuvered to keep Elizabeth between him and Danny. Often when he went to pick Elizabeth up, Danny was off somewhere else. But when they came home, Danny would be waiting. Robert still would walk Elizabeth to the door. As soon as she went inside, how he would run and jump back into his car. He would get butted but not very hard. Billie and Kathleen would watch through a window and just laugh and laugh. For some reason Robert only took Elizabeth out a few times, but he did pay special attention to her at church.

Lynn's dog, Scaramouch, slept in Lynn's room each night, but often Lynn would smuggle Danny down the stairs into his room as well. Danny and Scaramouch got along just fine. The dog and Lynn loved each other, but Danny was cuter than the dog.

It had become obvious that there was no way the Millers were going to be eating mutton from this source. He was nimble and would jump sideways when anyone went out to pay some attention to him. Danny also was quite smart and was soon opening gates and doors. One day, Kate had bought two big sacks of rabbit pellets and put them into the shed. She went back twice to make sure the door was closed. Mr. Sweeney, a person who was always coming by to see if they had extra eggs, chickens, rabbits, or anything else to sell, came by. Kate said, "No, we don't have anything today." Then she started toward the house. Oh, no! The shed door was open. "Wait a minute," she said, and she took off running.

Sure enough, there was Danny greedily eating several rabbits' portions of food. She took him by the back of his neck and led him out to Mr. Sweeney. "What will you give me for this guy?"

Mr. Sweeney scratched his head and reached into his pocket and pulled out eight dollars, "This is all I've got with me today."

Kate shoved Danny toward the buyer. "He's yours." And she reached over and took the money."

How she dreaded her family coming home that night! She had practically given Danny away. Lynn and Roy both knew that he was a pest, but they would miss him. The girls were a little sorry but they hardly noticed he was gone. Actually, they all took his being sold better than Kate thought they would.

Kate would buy four young turkeys a year. These she would turn loose in the yard to fend for themselves. She would put out some grain for them but mostly they found their own food. Some years they would be mean and go running up to people and peck them. Kate and Roy could turn them away with their voices. Billie would carry a broom or stick with her when she went outside. They would eat Kate's turkeys for Christmas and Thanksgiving and two other times a year.

Chapter 32

One summer the family went to visit the Miller relatives in Idaho. Roy's sister, Mary, had moved there, married Lovell McKillip, and had two sons named Dean and Lewis. Roy's brother Frank and his wife, Mary, had two sons named Bill and Scott. His brother Don and his wife, Rachel, lived there with their children. His sister, Florence, and her two children, Mary and Eddie, lived in Idaho, too. So off the family went.

During the visit, all the family went sight-seeing together in two cars. One of the cars got a flat tire. Repairing a tire usually meant about an hour of labor; taking the tire off the car, removing the inner tube, finding the hole, putting glue all around the hole, putting a patch on the hole, and rubbing and rubbing to make sure the patch would stay on and cover the hole completely and securely. Next the tube was replaced in the tire. Then came the hardest part of all: Roy would use a hand pump to replace the air that had escaped. He had to pump a very long time!

This time, everyone piled out of the car with the flat and all the men piled out of the other car. Frank came over and told Kate and the girls, "Just stay in the car, we'll be ready to go in a few minutes."

How could that be? There were a lot of men but the steps were the same and they would have to take turns.

But sure enough, in a few minutes here came Roy and Don. Everyone climbed back into the cars and off they went. Billie wondered how it was accomplished so quickly but she was much too shy to ask in front of all those people. Later she did ask her dad and he said, "Frank had an extra tire in his car already on a wheel. He just carries it around all ready to put on the car if one of his tires goes flat. He calls it a spare tire. So you just take off the flat one and put on the spare."

The next day, the family went into the corn field and picked ears of corn. The stalks were taller than the people and they could hardly see one another while they were picking. Kate, Roy, and the children took off for home the following morning with several ears of corn but they also had a big bucket of seed corn. They were going to plant it in one of the three fields.

They stored the seeds until it was time to plant the following year. Roy plowed the land into rows. Everyone had his or her own row. Each person took off walking. Everyone had a stick and a sack of seed corn. They would take a step or two, poke a hole with the stick, drop a seed in the hole, and then step on it to cover the seed. Unfortunately, no one could hit the hole standing up, so everyone walked all bent over. This was an uncommon way to walk and was quite exhausting. There was quite a bit of griping and whining. Finally, the corn was planted and a worn out family went back to the house. Kate had helped plant but now she also fixed supper. Roy had helped plant but he still had cows to milk. That evening everyone sat around and moaned.

Roy said, "It'll be worth it. Just think of all the wonderful corn we will be eating before too long."

The corn that had grown taller than a person in Idaho, grew about four feet high. In Idaho, the ears were twelve to fourteen inches long. In Mesa, the ears grew to be about six inches long. When they were picked, instead of corn there were dried kernels. It really wasn't edible. Apparently, it needed to be irrigated oftener than the alfalfa. So that fall the cows got to take a turn in the corn field. Even if it wasn't suitable for people, the cows liked it just fine.

Chapter 33

Kate had gone into the rabbit business. She would feed and water several pens of rabbits every morning. Many Monday mornings, between milking and school, Roy would kill and skin rabbits. Then Kate would cut them up to get them ready to sell to a local grocery store. Kate would then stretch the white fur and hang it on the clothesline to dry out and those she would mail to a fur company for the sum of thirty cents each.

One morning she went out and there was a big king snake lying in the sun with six very obvious bumps along his length. Sure enough, one of the nests was empty. He had eaten all the babies of one of the does. Kate got a hoe and killed the snake. She figured that now that he had a taste of baby rabbits, they wouldn't be safe from him anymore. As a rule, king snakes were not killed. Mice were a big problem and they were usually the snakes' main food, so they were usually considered helpful.

Because Kate had too much to do, she turned the rabbit business over to Lynn and Elizabeth. They fed and watered and cleaned and sprayed water on the lath house. In return, they made the rabbit money. After a few months, Elizabeth said, "I'm not making enough money for the work. I like babysitting much better." So Lynn did it alone.

One Christmas, Lynn got a B.B. gun. It seemed to be an extension of his arm. Never again did his sisters have to wonder what to buy him for birthdays and Christmas because they always knew they could buy him ammunition. How he loved to shoot his gun. His aim was terrific. He could shoot the head off a flying dragonfly. He was smart enough not to shoot bigger living things because he knew that would be the end of his having the gun for a while.

One year, Lynn saved his money and bought a .22 rifle from Sears and Roebuck. He and Roy would go cottontail hunting. For Billie's 16th birthday, he took her out to shoot rabbits. Sitting on the fender of the vehicle was great fun, finding the rabbits was exciting, but Billie had no desire to shoot the cute little things.

Grandpa Troyer would spend the winters with Kate and Roy's family. He had trouble staying warm and would mostly sit at the dining room table with a blanket around his shoulders. One summer, Kate and Billie were taking him back to Kate's sister, Lena, in Colorado. They had just gotten into the valley below Wolf Creek Pass, when the horn started blowing. They pulled over to the side of the road and raised the hood. Grandpa Troyer tried to find the wire that went to the horn. The noise was deafening. He pulled a wire. Nothing happened. He pulled another wire. Nothing happened. He pulled one wire after another until finally the noise stopped. Many of the wires under the hood were disconnected. It was evening and they were right by a motel so Kate went and got rooms. The next morning she was certain the car would not start, but start it did. They drove into Pueblo to Kate's brother, Mose's house. All were relieved to get there. They spent a couple of hours visiting and went out to get into the car. When Kate tried to start the car, it didn't make a sound. Instead, Mose drove them to Lena's house and said he would see about getting the car fixed. If the car was ever fixed, Kate did not know it. She and Billie took the train back to Mesa.

Chapter 34

Almost every Saturday, the five children went to the only theater in town. They almost always had a double feature and the movies were quite entertaining. They would go no matter what was on, but the three oldest loved the musicals. Lynn liked the westerns and Kathleen liked them all. For children under twelve, the price was thirteen cents, and for those over twelve, the price was thirty-five cents. Ann was small for her age, but Billie had a great growth spurt when she was ten and so was tall for her age. The prices were higher for twelve-year-olds, and the ticket sellers always thought Ann was not yet twelve and Billie was already twelve. To simplify things, Ann started buying Billie's ticket and Billie would buy Ann's. Ann was baby-sitting quite a bit so she could afford the higher price while Billie couldn't. Elizabeth and Ann began babysitting to make money starting on their twelfth birthdays until they could get other jobs at the age of sixteen. As they quit because they had other jobs, Billie took over their customers.

Elizabeth was on the school tennis team and would go to school soon after daylight to practice. She and Doris Fennison traded being first and second on the Mesa High School tennis team. She was good enough so that she had her first year of college at ASC in Tempe paid for with a tennis scholarship. Then she found that they expected her to play tennis several hours each day. She felt she was not good enough to go pro and was not willing to spend so much time playing tennis. Because of that, she still played tennis during her sophomore year, but she was on a work study program and had to work at various jobs at the college as well.

Her junior year, Elizabeth went to Bob Jones University. Kate had made all of the girls squaw dresses. They had tiers and very full skirts. They were decorated with lots of rickrack and were very popular in Arizona. In South Carolina, at Bob Jones University, the only time Elizabeth wore it was on Halloween night. While at Bob Jones' University, Elizabeth still played tennis. She even won a tennis competition, and the school was rewarded with the trophy.

There was a hepatitis scare while she was there. But every student got shots to prevent them from catching it so there was no epidemic as at first feared. Elizabeth said there were two things that got you into trouble at Bob Jones University: complaining and lying. She joked, "If you complained about the food you were in trouble. If you said the food was good, you were in trouble for lying." After that year at Bob Jones University, she came back and graduated from Arizona State College in Tempe.

When Ann turned sixteen, her first job was at the theater. She no longer got to see the movies in full, but she did see bits and pieces of all of them. She was an avid reader and thought that movies were quite repetitious. She said she always knew how they would end. After working there awhile, she went to work as a cook for a small restaurant. It was much harder work but the pay was better. She met a lot of people and some of her customers became aware of her intelligence.

During her senior year of high school, Ann was offered the job as women's society editor of the Mesa Tribune. The next year Ann was a freshman at ASC and Elizabeth was a sophomore. They drove to Tempe as early as classes were available. Both were taking full loads, and then they were home by three o'clock in the afternoon to begin work. Ann worked on the Tribune and Elizabeth had a job typing through the college.

Billie had found a job the summer she was sixteen at Mesa Drug as a soda jerk. What fun! The same people came in everyday and she thought it was quite wonderful. She had spent two days looking for a job and then her dad had gotten Paul Schlinghoff, a fellow Elk member, to give her a chance. He was the manager of the fountain at Mesa Drug. The job was the most fun she had ever had in her life, plus she was getting paid. It was the first time that she had fellowship with people outside of church and school and she found to her surprise that most people are nice and fun.

She worked at the fountain for two years. One day, she asked a fellow worker, Uldean, if she wanted to go to the movie down the street. Uldean replied, "I'll take a rain check on that." Even though she was an avid reader, Billie had no idea what Uldean meant.

Another time, Billie was told to peel twenty pounds of potatoes for the next day, which she did. Her boss had not told her to cover them with water after she peeled them, and he was quite angry at the ugly looking potatoes the next day. Many had to be peeled again.

Billie happily took the unpleasant jobs; sorting rotten and not rotten potatoes, cleaning the syrupy coke machine whenever it emptied, cleaning the grill, and washing the mirrors behind the counter. The coke machine was the worst. At that time, whenever a person ordered a coke, the waitress would put in one squirt of coke and fill the glass with carbonated water. So a couple of times a week, she would clean the machine before pouring the concentrated syrup into the machine.

Billie had led a very sheltered life and several times did not catch on to a joke or know what fellow workers were talking about. She knew sometimes they teased her, but it was friendly teasing. She worked there for two years, then Helen Duckworth, the owner, came to her and asked her if she was interested in learning how to keep books. Of course, Billie jumped at the chance. She learned how to pay the bills and write the checks and count up the day's receipts. She would never finish until the bank was closed so she would walk across the two streets and put the money in the night deposit. The bank was cattycorner from the drugstore.

Her first job every day after school was to go to the window of the bank and retrieve the bag and make the deposit officially from the take of the day before. The teller hated to see her come. Most window transactions were simple. These deposits were quite complicated and time consuming. This job was interesting but the camaraderie was missing.

When Billie graduated from high school, she received a scholarship to Arizona State College in Tempe for the following semester. Helen Duckworth was a member of a woman's club that gave the scholarship. She knew Billie was a hard worker.

But Billie was not perfect. Every year at Christmas, the Duckworths gave their employees a bonus. They would add the bonus to their regular pay and figure the taxes and then pay them their regular salaries with just a little extra tax taken out. At the Christmas party they would give out the bonus checks. Billie knew the drill but she forgot to subtract the bonus from one of the clerk's checks. The clerk went to Dave Duckworth, the owner of the drugstore and the pharmacist, and showed her check with the bonus amount on it.

Dave said, "Thank you, I'll take care of it." He took the check and had Billie make out a new one. Then he gave the clerk her regular salary and scolded Billie for several minutes.

The Duckworths were rather stand-offish with their help, except at the Christmas party. Then they were just two of the guys. Mrs. Duckworth was overweight but she had been a champion swimmer and was able to move around very well. On the night of the Christmas party she would dance as often as everyone and she would do the Charleston at least once during the night.

Chapter 35

When Lynn started high school and Kathleen was in sixth grade, Kate went to work at the school cafeteria. For the first time in her married life she had money without having to ask Roy. She bought things needed for the house and for herself. The fun was that she could spend as she wished without explaining why she wanted the money. She loved the job. She had friends outside of the church. She was working with other adults. For the first time in her life she was working for money she could spend exactly as she wished. She really enjoyed her job and the camaraderie of the other workers.

Ann, Elizabeth, and Billie were all going to ASC in Tempe. Liz was a senior, Ann a junior, and Billie was a freshman. They lived at home and shared a ride to Tempe in a Willy's jeepster that Roy and Kate had bought for that purpose. They were all paying their own way to college. On the night of homecoming, the university gave away a blanket to the parent who had the most children enrolled in the college. Apparently, you had to apply to get it, because Kate did not receive the blanket. The mother who got it had two children enrolled at the time and one who had graduated. Kate was quite disappointed.

Lynn struggled in school. He was often in trouble. One of his teachers pulled his hair when he made a mistake, so Roy shaved his head at Lynn's suggestion. Kate and Roy knew that Lynn knew the information. Roy would drill him and drill him before a test. That night he knew the answers, the next day he would fail the test.

Outside of school, Lynn was a happy boy. He and Roy were good friends. They milked the cows. They went hunting and fishing, and now Lynn had a rifle and could go shooting whenever he had the money for shells.

Kathleen had no trouble in school. She was popular and happy. She did have periods of time when she would stare off into space. She would not hear Kate when she talked to her during this time. Finally, Kate took her to the doctor.

After the examination the doctor said, "She hasn't started her period yet. I can't find anything wrong with her. I expect it is just hormones. When she starts her period, the spells should stop."

Kate took the doctor's word for it and they went home. Kathleen didn't seem to be in any pain and the spells didn't happen that often.

Kate was well satisfied with her life. Her mother had died and her father would spend the winters in the small bedroom off the screened-in porch. He was a quiet, agreeable man. He had asked Kate to give him his insulin shots but she had refused. He did it himself for the first time. Sarah had always done it for him.

Kathleen and Lynn would spend time with Grandpa Troyer when they came home from school before doing their homework. He was always cold, so they would meet in the kitchen because it was warmer.

Grandpa Troyer liked taking Lynn fishing, and Lynn enjoyed going with him. One day Lynn caught a sucker about twelve inches long. Grandpa scooped up some lake water and put the fish in a pail. Then they went home. Grandpa showed the fish to Kate and then he went and ran water and put it in the only bathtub. Kate objected but he just said, "Just 'til everyone sees it. Just 'til everyone sees it."

As the girls came home from various places he led each one to see the huge fish Lynn had caught. He had Kate find her cloth measuring tape and they measured it. He wrote a letter to the folks back home. Lynn was proud as punch and a little amused at Grandpa making a big deal about the fish.

That summer when it was time for Grandpa to go back to Colorado, Roy and Grandpa took turns driving Grandpa's model A car. Lynn went along for the ride. It was such fun riding with the two men he loved. They had a great trip. They rode over Wolf Creek Pass. The car would strain a good deal going up those steep hills. Then it would take off smoothly and quickly going down the hills. They ate breakfast in restaurants. That was a new experience for Lynn. They also talked. Lynn listened intently to the men as they told fishing stories and stories about when they first met and Roy was just a little older than Lynn was now.

This year they couldn't stay long. Kate was home milking the cows and it wasn't fair to take longer than necessary. So after two nights and one day of visiting, they headed for the train station. What a ride that was! Lynn walked all over the train. He liked the observation car, and getting water for them to drink, and the toilet on the train, and eating in the dining car. He was so happy to be traveling with his dad.

In the winter, Roy would teach, Kate would work in the cafeteria, and Lynn and Kathleen went to school. Elizabeth had graduated from Arizona State College in Tempe and now had a teaching job in Prescott. Ann was working for the Mesa Tribune and selling advertisement for the newspaper at ASC. She was working toward her journalist degree. Billie was working at Mesa Drug and taking bookkeeping classes at ASC. All of the family except Elizabeth were still living at home.

Kathleen once again started staring off into space. Then one day Kate felt her forehead, and found that Kathleen felt warm, so Kate took her temperature. Kathleen had a 104 degree temperature. So off they went to the doctor. The doctor scolded Kate for not bringing her in sooner. Kate was given a prescription to get filled.

The doctor said, "Salt is her enemy. You need to keep her off salt until she gets over this kidney infection. Be sure and give her this medicine until she gets over this. I want to see her in a week."

Kate stopped and got the medicine. Then she got to thinking about what he had said, 'salt is her enemy'. She went home and made bread without salt. She was careful to cook without salt. The others could put on salt as they wanted.

Kathleen was wonderful. She didn't like the way the food tasted without salt, but she had been there when the doctor had scolded her mother. She took her medicine and ate everything salt free.

Three nights after going to the doctor, Kathleen woke up with terrible cramps in her legs. Roy and Kate massaged her legs until the cramps went away. She went back to sleep. Unfortunately, the cramps kept coming back.

Kate called the doctor. She said, "We're doing what you said. We haven't missed one time of giving her the medicine. I am cooking without salt. I am even baking bread without salt."

The doctor said, "She has to have some salt. That is why she is getting these cramps. Give her some quinine and just cut down on the salt. Don't cut it out completely."

Kate got the quinine. It helped. But she stewed about the way the doctor had talked to her both times. Why didn't he say cut down on the salt instead of 'salt is your enemy?' Kathleen eventually got over the kidney infection.

Chapter 36

In the summer, Kate, Roy, Lynn and Kathleen would go to Colorado to visit his parents and Kate's brothers and sister. This was always a happy time. Lewis had retired and there was an article in the local newspaper;

RESIGNS MENNONITE
CHURCH PASSTORATE
The Rev. Dr. Lewis C. Miller for the past 17 years pastor of the Mennonite Church at Manitou Springs, and the last two years at 22nd and Kiowa in Colorado Springs, resigned his pastorate be- cause of the health condition both of himself and his wife. The resignation was accepted by the bishop of the congregation at a special service last Sunday night. Dr. Miller has served the Mennonite Church as an unsalaried minister for 18 years. In this time he had only two pastorates, one of 11 years from 1922 to 1933 at Limon, Colorado and the other from 1933 to 1950 in Manitou and Colorado Springs. Dr. and Mrs. Miller will continue to reside at 206 Deerpath Avenue, Manitou Springs.

During his work in the ministry the two congregations increased in membership under Dr. Miller,

from 19 charter members, to an all time high of 118 at Limon, and from a membership of 41 to an all time high of 118 at Colorado Springs and Manitou Springs Church.

Lewis and Susie lived in a house on a hill in Manitou Springs. Lewis took Roy aside and said, "If something happens to me first, I want you to take care of your Mother."

Roy said, "You know I will."

His mother said, "Promise me I won't have to go into a county home."

Roy said, "I promise."

Then Grandpa Miller started wandering. He would leave home and have to be found. One day he walked downtown and stood in the middle of the road of Manitou Springs and shouted, "I own this town. This is my town."

He was removed by force and it became necessary to put him in a place of safety. He went into the Old Soldiers' Home. He liked it pretty well and fit right in. Grandma Miller was moved in with a friend.

It was during these trips to Colorado that they would take Kate's father back and leave him with Lena and Ora for the summer. It was so much fun to visit Lena, Perry, Mose, and their families. Lynn and Kathleen got to know their cousins a little. The three older girls had jobs and went to summer school and did not feel they could make the trips.

While the three older daughters were in college, they were basically paying their own tuition and buying the gas to go back and forth. They would come home to sleep and eat. When all five children were at home, Roy always had to work most of the summer. When all three girls had been in college for a year, Roy and Kate decided to move from Palmer's. He wanted more rent and having cows and all these animals made traveling difficult.

They found the house they liked. They rented it for a year with an option to buy it at the end of that year. They liked that idea. They could decide whether or not this was the house they wanted. After they had moved in, they began working on the place. They put in plants and got the lawn looking really nice. Then they went to the landlord and told them they would repaint inside and out if he would buy the paint. He bought the paint. Kate worked on their new home. It kept looking nicer and nicer.

On the first night the family spent in the new home, Billie went on a date with a barber who ate in the drugstore where she had been working at the lunch counter. By the time he finally asked her out, she had moved from the lunch counter to the office upstairs. She would pay the bills and count the day's receipts and even make out the payroll.

For their date, they went to a double feature movie in Phoenix. Billie was nervous all evening. He was so handsome and so smart and so worldly. He had been in the Navy for almost four years and had traveled a lot with his parents. She was also nervous because she wasn't sure that she would recognize the house that her parents had moved into. Because she had been so busy with school and work, she had not helped them move at all. She didn't know the address, she only knew which street. He would think she was an idiot when she didn't know where she lived. Fortunately, by the time he took her home everyone else was home and she recognized the cars in the driveway. What a relief!

Elizabeth had graduated and moved to Prescott to teach school. While there she met a carpenter and house builder named Frank at church one day. This was fine with Elizabeth. She loved living in Prescott. It was a nice place and there was a lot of building going on. They fell in love and planned to marry in June of 1955.

Things went as planned and they wed in the Baptist Church in Mesa. She had showers at both churches, the one in Mesa and the one in Prescott. She had a lingerie shower by the friends she made at school and at work in Mesa. She had another shower by the teachers in Prescott. She got many wonderful gifts. She had a huge wedding and got many gifts there, too.

Kate made Elizabeth a long white gown. She had a beautiful wedding in the First Baptist Church in Mesa. She walked down the aisle on her Dad's arm. She was married by Rev. Kmetko.

Then instead of being able to take a breath, Kate and Billie went shopping for material to make her third daughter a dress. They finally found a beautiful blue iridescent material. Kate sewed it and made a slip to match. Billie wanted a dress she could wear over and over again. Unfortunately, the material split when it was cleaned so that she could not wear it again.

Herb and Billie had decided to get married, but he made it quite plain that he was not going for any big wedding. They decided to go to Las Vegas. Billie refused to go before Elizabeth's wedding because she didn't want people saying she ran away to get married so she could get married before Elizabeth. So over the long Fourth of July weekend, they took off for Las Vegas.

There were lots of places to get married but Kate had asked Billie to find a Baptist Preacher and have him perform the ceremony. She thought it would be more spiritual. They got into town quite early in the morning and set off to buy Billie a ring.

Herb said, "We can't afford it."

Billie said, "We have to afford it. I want a ring."

They found a small store run by a Jew. There were two rings and Billie couldn't make up her mind. One was just a simple band of gold. The other one was much wider and had some etching on it. As she fluctuated between the two, the Jewish owner kept coming down on the simple band. When he got down to four dollars, Billie said, "We'll take it."

When she and Herb were outside Herb said, "I didn't know you knew enough to bargain with a Jew. They really think they are to make the first sale of the week or they will have a bad week."

Billie wasn't smart enough to say thanks. She said, "I wasn't bargaining. I just couldn't make up my mind."

They stood in line for three hours to get a license. When they got up to the window, the clerk wouldn't sell them one because he wasn't sure that Billie was eighteen years old. She had left her purse in the car.

He said, "When you get your driver's license just come on up to my window. You don't have to get at the end of the line."

So off they went back to the car. It was about a mile away and when they got back to the courthouse it had closed for lunch. So they went and ate lunch, too.

Billie had found a phone booth and called a Baptist Preacher and made arrangements for him to marry them at 3:00. Then back they went to the courthouse and went to the head of the line and the clerk looked at her identification and sold them a license. Then they drove around and found the preacher's house. They got there close to the time and rang the bell.

He may have been a preacher but he was rude. "Where are your witnesses?" was the way he greeted them when he opened the door.

Billie said, "We don't have any"

"Oh, well, I guess I can find someone." The preacher went into the other room and had a man and a young child come into the room. Billie and Herb stood in front of the preacher. The man and child sat on the couch in the room and he read the Sunday comics to the youngster.

The ceremony was short and sweet. The smallest bill they had was a twenty, and even though they thought he deserved less they gave it to him and left. They walked around Las Vegas since Billie was too young to gamble and rented a room for the night. They headed home on the Fourth of July and took up residence in the small apartment behind Joe's Barbershop where Herb worked.

Chapter 38

One night Roy finished paying the bills. As he walked past Kate, he stopped and waved an envelope. "This is it, the last payment on the Desoto."

Kate turned and looked at him, "That's too bad. I really like that car."

Roy said, "We still have the car, but now it is paid for."

Kate smiled, "You've always said, 'I'll always have a car payment.' As soon as you pay a car off, you trade it in,"

Roy grinned, "Not this time. I like this car, too."

Kate's smile got bigger. "Won't that be great? Just like getting a raise."

One Saturday, soon after that conversation, the phone rang. Ann was on the phone. "Mom, I'm sorry, I wrecked the car. Could you come and get me?"

Wrecked the car! But wait! It's not too bad. Ann is on the phone. She must be all right. "Of course, we'll come. Where are you?"

Ann told her.

"We'll be there as soon as we can. You know it will be awhile but we are on our way."

Roy and Kate stopped at Rendezvous Park where Kathleen was swimming to make sure she had a place to go afterwards. Her friend said, "My mom is going to pick me up. She can go over to our house." Kate told Kathleen they would stop and pick her up on the way home.

Ann was waiting by the phone booth. She was a little dirty and her crooked glasses gave her a bedraggled look. The first thing she said was, "I'm so sorry about the car."

Roy said, "No problem, as long as you're all right. Can you tell us what happened?"

Ann said, "I decided to go up on South Mountain to make some decisions. It always seems like I can think better when I am up high. On the way up, I had a sneezing spell and my glasses fell off. I was groping for my glasses and I drove off the road. I crashed through the railing and must have stopped close to the road. I couldn't start the car again so I climbed out of the car and was flagging down a car in a minute or two. I had the driver bring me down to the phone and I called you."

"Do you think the car is all right where it is?" Roy asked.

"Probably, the guy that picked me up said he didn't see my car so it must be out of sight from the road pretty well."

Roy called a towing company, told them where the car was, and asked the driver to get his car the next day. The driver called him back later that day. "That car is there to stay. There is no way to get it out of there." Since the car was paid off, there was no insurance on it. Roy had another car he was driving and they decided to go without a second car until they came back from their yearly trip to Colorado.

Kate said, "What will Ann do?" She has a job and is going to summer school in Tempe. She has to have a car."

Ann was dating a boy named Freddie. She reassured her parents, "Don't worry about me. Freddie is going out of town with his folks and has loaned me his car until school starts in the fall. You will be back by then. Freddie wants to get married but I'm not sure that's what I want. I really like and respect him, but I'm not sure I love him,"

Billie and Herb decided to go see where the Desoto was. They couldn't believe their eyes. The car had broken through the railing and dropped straight down. It was on a very narrow ledge about fifty feet below the road. It looked impossible to climb. The side of the drop was very straight and seemed very smooth.

When Billie saw Ann again, she asked how she got back up to the road.

Ann answered, "I remember getting out of the car. Then I was by the side of the road flagging down a car. The first car that came by stopped and took me to the phone I used to call Mom."

Billie said to Herb, "I think her guardian angel was looking after her."

Herb just raised his eyebrows but he kept his opinion to himself.

Chapter 39

Kate, Roy, Lynn, and Kathleen took off for their yearly trip back to see Roy's parents and to visit the rest of the families in Colorado. Since they planned to be in Colorado for two months, the two adults knew they needed to go job hunting. Grandpa Miller was in the Old Soldiers' Home, and Susie was now staying in a hotel room where someone cleaned her rooms and brought her meals to her. Since Manitou Springs was so busy in the summer, the hotel was happy to hire Kate to clean rooms and help with laundry. Roy and Lynn got jobs in a furniture store. Kathleen spent her days with Grandma Miller.

Kathleen decided to take good care of Grandma while she was with her. She served her breakfast and lunch, brought her water, and read to her. Sometimes Grandma Miller would take naps and then Kathleen would read and have time to herself, but she was literally at her Grandma's beck and call.

Grandma Miller loved Lynn. She often gave him small gifts and lots of praise. The only time she acknowledged Kathleen was when she wanted something.

At least once a week, Kate and Kathleen would walk downtown in Manitou Springs. They would window shop and have a lemonade in a small café. It was on one of these jaunts when Kathleen asked, "Why doesn't Grandma Miller like me?"

Kate thought a minute, "Old people often don't like the person taking care of them. I guess they are really unhappy with their own lack of ability but take it out on the caregiver."

Kathleen brightened. "So maybe she likes me okay. What she really doesn't like is being helpless."

Kate smiled. Kathleen was a wonderful, intuitive child. "That's it exactly."

While they were in Colorado, they had a wonderful time visiting. Kathleen became a teenager on August 17. One day, they went to a park for a picnic. Lynn and Kathleen were playing hide-and-seek. Kathleen was crouched at the end of a fallen tree that was at least twelve inches in diameter. Lynn was walking on the tree looking for Kathleen. As Lynn walked to the end, Kathleen sat up fast and bumped her head on the very end of the tree. It was lower because Lynn was walking on it. Lynn felt the whole tree shudder after a terrible thump. Lynn was so afraid that Kathleen was badly hurt. Lynn had been knocked senseless by a cow the month before and he thought Kathleen's bump was harder than his had been. Kathleen insisted that she was just fine.

That same afternoon, Roy and Kathleen were walking through the woods. Roy was leading and he let a branch go and heard a thump. He turned and saw that the branch had hit Kathleen in the forehead.

Roy said, "Kathleen, I'm so sorry. I didn't realize that you were right behind me."

Kathleen said, "It's all right. It didn't hurt very much." Then they walked back to camp.

When Kate heard about the mishaps, she made sure that Kathleen stayed awake and watched her. She seemed to be doing fine. A few days later they headed back to Mesa. School would start soon and they wanted to be back a few days before they had to go back to work.

As they were driving home, Kathleen complained about a headache. Then Kathleen went into convulsions. Remembering the blows to her head, Kate and Roy rushed her to the hospital. By the time they got there she seemed to be much better. The doctor who looked at her said, "Go on home and take her to a doctor there. He will probably have to run tests to see what the problem is." So the next morning they headed to Mesa.

When they got to Mesa, it was about 4:00 on a Thursday afternoon. Kate called her doctor's office. The receptionist said the earliest they could get in was the following Monday. Kate insisted that was too late. They had been on the road for two days and it was imperative that the doctor see Kathleen now. She had not had any more seizures but she would get a vacant look in her eyes and be off in another place. She also had complained of headaches. Finally, after much insisting Kate made an appointment for Friday.

When they got to the doctor's office and Kate described the things that had taken place, the doctor put Kathleen into the Mesa Hospital for tests and observation. That night Kate stayed with her and the next day the tests started. There were several tests taken and Kate stayed with Kathleen as much as they would let her. In 1955 tests were quite hard on a person physically. Kathleen became more and more fatigued.

When Herb took Billie to see her, Kathleen recognized Billie's voice but she did not turn her head to look at her. Billie bent over the bed and looked at her little sister since Kathleen was lying on her back and looking straight up.

Billie said, "How are you feeling?"

Kathleen's voice was low, "I don't hurt. I'm just very, very tired."

Billie said, "At least you're in the right place. They'll look after you."

They only stayed a few minutes as Kathleen was obviously exhausted and kept closing her eyes as though to go to sleep.

Finally, they finished giving the tests but then they had to wait to get the results. Kate was in the hospital day and night. She just slept in the chair next to her daughter. Finally, the doctor came in with the results. "It's good news. There seems to be nerve damage. She is going to do just fine."

Kate and Roy conversed, and Roy said, "Isn't there a nerve specialist you could call."

The doctor said, "Usually the person just has to take her time recovering. There isn't a lot that can be done to help her get better."

Kate insisted, "We want a nerve specialist called in."

When the doctor saw how serious they were, he said, "Actually, Mesa has a very fine nerve specialist. I'll put in the call."

The nerve specialist did come and look at the tests and examine Kathleen. He agreed with Dr. Cline. "In cases like these, the patient will pull through. It is a slow process but when they begin healing, you notice differences every day. Just be patient and let her heal at her own pace. We'll keep her here in the hospital a few more days." Then he looked at Kate. "We'll take care of her. You go home and get a good night's sleep."

Kate said, "I want to stay with her again tonight. I'll sleep just as good in this chair as I will at home in bed."

Doctor Cline said, "You won't rest as well. Now you go home, doctor's orders."

Roy took Kate's arm. "You know they'll take care of her. Come on. Let's go home."

Kate didn't want to go but she was terribly tired, so she and Roy went home.

They got a call from the hospital very early in the morning telling them to come down immediately. Fearing the worst, they were dressed and a few minutes after getting the call they were pulling into the hospital parking lot. It was the worst. Kathleen had passed away during the night. Kate thought her heart would break.

Roy was incredulous. "You told us she would be all right. What happened? Why did she die?"

The doctor said, "We don't know. She shouldn't have died. The only way to find out what happened is to perform an autopsy."

Kate said, "No! I don't want her cut up."

Roy said, "We have to know why she died."

Kate was adamant. "No!"

The doctor led Kate and Roy into his office. "She shouldn't have died. If we do an autopsy maybe the next little girl or boy won't die, because we'll know more."

Kate knew Kathleen was no longer in that body. They were right. No one should have to go through this agony. With tears streaming down her face, she agreed.

Kate and Roy went home. They had to notify people. Lynn and Ann were still at home so they were told first and then Billie was called by her dad. He said, "Your sister passed away in her sleep last night. I have to call other people. Maybe you want to come over to the house."

Billie said, "Have you called Elizabeth?"

Roy said, "No, she doesn't even know that Kathleen was in the hospital. We were going to wait and tell her after she was better."

Herb had been listening in on the phone call. He said, "We'll drive to Prescott and tell her."

Roy said, "That would be great," And he hung up.

Billie and Herb drove their 1950 Mercury to Prescott. At that time the way to go was through Wickenburg. When they got to the apartment in Granite Dells, north of Prescott, Herb took over. Elizabeth was glad to see them. She had put a roast with potatoes and carrots in a pot on the stove early in the morning. She said that Frank would be home for lunch in about an hour.

Herb said, "Let's go get him."

Now Elizabeth was nervous, but off the three of them went. Frank had just finished saying, "We should keep our wives at home barefoot and pregnant," when he saw his pregnant wife walking across the field in her bare feet. He was surprised when he saw that she was with Billie and Herb, so he quit what he was doing and went over to the car. "What's up?"

Herb said, "We need to go back to the house."

Frank could see that something was unusual, so he immediately got into his car. They went back to the apartment and then Herb said to Billie, "You have to tell them."

Billie had counted on Herb telling them so she just blurted out. "Kathleen died in her sleep last night."

Elizabeth was flabbergasted. Then Billie told her everything she knew, which was very little.

Frank said, "We'll follow you back in our car."

Elizabeth gave the roast to her landlord that lived in the other part of the building and they took off.

The next few days were a haze. Some of Roy's and Kate's brothers and sisters came for the funeral and then they were gone.

Kathleen died on Labor Day, the 7th of September. The year's lease for the house was up on the 15th of September. They had already notified their landlord that they would buy the house when the lease was up. They had the money and they could not concern themselves about it until the 15th.

On the 8th of September, their landlord came by and said, "We've decided to move back into the house. You need to be out by the 15th." Of course the landlords would want to live there; Kate and Roy's care made the house so much nicer than it had been when they moved in.

Kate said, "No way. We need until the first of October."

The wife then said, "You'll have to pay more rent for the extra two weeks."

Again Kate said, "No way."

Roy went back to teaching the following Monday and Lynn started school. Kate went back to the school cafeteria. But she was barely functioning. At night she would pack things in boxes so that they could move at the first of the month. When Kate was home, she dearly missed Kathleen. Of her daughters, Kathleen was her best friend. When Kathleen was growing up, Kate had been at a time of her life when she was not as busy and as stressed as when her three oldest daughters had been very young. Lynn and Roy had been good friends and Kate and Kathleen had been good friends.

Then the results of the autopsy came. Kathleen had choked to death. Kate was so unhappy. If she had stayed at the hospital that night, Kathleen probably would not have died. She was even more depressed. There was also further news. It had not been nerve damage that had cause Kathleen's problems. She had had a brain tumor. With all of this distressing news, Kate would get dressed, go to work, come home, and fix supper, but there was no joy in her life.

Chapter 40

They had to move by the end of the month, so Kate went apartment hunting. She found an apartment. Kate, Roy, Ann, and Lynn put their things into boxes and only took out the few things they needed. They knew they would go house hunting sometime in the future.

One day Ann came to Kate and said that she and Bill McDonough had decided to get married in November. She had met Bill at a function as he was working for the Chamber of Commerce for Mesa and she was there to write about what was happening for the paper. She knew that she loved him and not Freddie. She would take care of all the arrangements but she hoped her Mom and Dad would be there.

Kate said, "Of course, we will."

As the day of the wedding approached, Roy had further bad news. His Dad, Lewis Miller, had passed away. Of course, Kate and Roy would have to go to Colorado, so Ann and Bill postponed the wedding.

Kate and Roy went to Colorado. They made arrangements for his mom, Susie, to continue to stay in the hotel where she had been staying. They made sure someone would bring her meals and clean and check on her. Susie grabbed Roy's hand. "Promise me you won't put me into the county home." Roy promised again. They went back to Mesa to work.

When the new year started, Kate once again went house hunting. She found a house that they could afford if they were careful with their finances. Roy and Kate would work, eat, read, watch television and go to church. They didn't spend much money. They bought the house on Dana Street and moved into it. Kate planted a tree in the backyard and called it Kathleen's tree.

In April, Ann married Bill McDonough. Kate was in a whirl. Ann knew that Billie had not had a big wedding and she asked her to be a bride's maid. Billie wore her wedding dress and Ann had bought a light blue dress. It was a nice wedding. She, like Elizabeth, was married by Reverend Steve Kmetko in the First Baptist Church of Mesa. The reception was at another hall and Herb said to Billie, "You don't have to go there. They won't even miss you." Billie wanted to go but she also wanted to please Herb so she didn't go to the reception. No one ever said a word about her not being there.

The next weeks were terrible for Kate. She had been a member of the First Baptist Church for years, but she had always been a Sunday school teacher. She knew many of the young people at church but had not made many adult women friends. When she went to prayer meeting on Wednesday nights, Roy was at the Elks club playing poker. Her four children went with her, but again she did not really visit with other adults. Her house had been full of daughters, but then there were none. Lynn was still at home, but he was sixteen years old and she seldom saw him. When he wanted to talk to a parent it was Roy he went to, just as Kathleen had gone to Kate.

One weekend Lynn went out with his friends, Robbie Robson and Perry Tribbey, to go get honey from a hollow tree where one of them had seen a beehive. Out they went taking a welder's mask with them. They drew straws and Lynn had the short straw.

Robbie and Perry stripped down to their shorts and Lynn covered himself with their clothes. Over the welder's mask, he put one of their t-shirts as an extra protection. Then he took a bucket and dipper to get the honey while his friends cheered him on from a distance.

How the bees buzzed around. Lynn dipped honey. Bees buzzed. Then he felt a sting on the back of his neck. He grabbed the bucket and took off running as he hit the back of his neck. It was true about bees sending messages. An arm of the t-shirt was open at the back of his neck and several bees found that hole and stung him.

The three boys piled into the car and took Lynn home. He was in serious pain. When Kate heard what had happened, she was angry. Instead of sympathy, she snapped at Lynn, "If you insist on hurting yourself, don't come to me looking for sympathy."

A few months later, Kate heard an agonizing cry. Lynn had a burn on his hand.

Lynn said, "I need to go to see a doctor."

Again Kate's reaction was anger. But she took him to the emergency room. She went to the desk and said, "My son burned his arm. He thinks he needs to see a doctor."

The nurse looked at Lynn's arm and took him back immediately. Then she came back and told Kate, "He definitely needed to see a doctor. The pain must have been unbearable."

Lynn never told the doctor or his parents that he had been trying to blow up a red ant hill using a glass pill bottle filled with black powder and red phosphorous, and it had blown up in his hand.

How Kate's conscience bothered her, she had reacted in anger and not shown any care at all, but she suffered silently. She knew she should go to Lynn and apologize but she couldn't make herself do it. Her daughters were all gone and Lynn seemed to be on the road to destruction.

Kate went through the motions of living. At one point, she and Roy went fishing in the White Mountains and had a restful time. When they got home and opened their trunk to take in the camping gear, a skunk jumped out of the trunk and ran down the street. That made her smile since the smell was minimal, considering what it could have been had the animal been unhappy.

Scaramouch had adjusted to having little space to run around in at the smaller house. After all, he was eleven years old. They had tied a rag to the bottom of the screen door at the bedroom entrance, so he could grab it and go in the house whenever he wished even if they were gone. They would laugh when they turned the corner a block from the house and saw the young neighbor children petting and climbing on the big German shepherd. When he recognized the car, he would stand up and start barking. How the children would scatter. By the time they got to the driveway, there were no children to be seen.

When the milkman delivered milk and they were sitting at the kitchen table, Scaramouch would bark energetically. Then Roy, Kate, or Lynn would hold his collar while the milkman put the milk in the refrigerator. One morning they all had to leave before the milkman had come. They figured there would be no fresh milk in the refrigerator that night. But it was there just as usual.

On the next delivery date, as Kate held barking Scaramouch's collar, Roy said, "Weren't you afraid to come in with no one here?"

The milkman grinned. "He never even got up when I came in. He just looked at me and went back to sleep."

Kate spent time praying and reading her Bible. She said to Billie one time, "God must want children in heaven, too. Wouldn't it be sad if there were no children there?"

Her life was so empty. Lynn and Roy were busy even when they were at home. She went to work at the school cafeteria and was glad for her job. Billie had had a daughter and named her Katherine Marie and sometimes they came over. But a baby was not the same as her own daughter. Nothing filled the void in her life.

Chapter 41

The summer of 1958 came. Roy got a summer job driving for General Motors. His position was checking tires and checking to see how the new cars held up over constant driving. It was one of the best and easiest jobs he had had in the summer. Every morning he would get in the new Chevy and drive through Wickenburg to Las Vegas. He would eat lunch and drive back. He enjoyed driving and mostly it was not difficult. He had been told never to exceed the speed limit but to drive right at it. This caused problems sometimes when he would get behind a big truck or some other vehicle going five miles or more under the speed limit. It was a two lane highway and he would need a long stretch of clearance before he could pass. He really didn't even mind that. It made the trip more interesting,

One day Kate got a phone call. Roy had been in a car wreck and was in the Wickenburg hospital. Lynn drove her to Wickenburg. Roy's car and the other car had each been over the line about a foot when they had crashed. The woman and child in the other car had died as a result of the accident. Roy was very seriously hurt. He was on the critical list for several days. He decided to live.

Then the operations started. He had pins put in his arms and he had to have false teeth put in. His jaw had been crushed and it was very difficult to fit his broken mouth and very painful for him to use his new teeth. He had always been a slim man. Whenever he would put on a few pounds, he would live on coffee and cigarettes until he lost them. Now even though he had no pounds to lose, he still lost weight.

Besides the damage that could be seen and fixed there was the additional damage of severe, agonizing headaches and other constant pain. It was very close to the end of the summer when the accident happened and the school season started without him. General Motors paid his hospital bills but that was all the money he received. Since he seldom missed school he had several sick days coming, so he was still receiving money from the school district to pay his other bills. Roy went to a lawyer to see if he could get some other compensation. It was a slow process. His lawyer told him he would keep him posted.

For the first time in her life, Kate took over the finances. She took his endorsed paycheck to the bank and wrote checks for the bills. She wanted to stay home with him but he insisted that she go back to work. The only thing he wanted to do was rest anyway. While she was at work, Roy found that taking alcohol relieved some of the pain. Soon it took more and more to relieve the pain. Then the school superintendent told him that if he wanted to keep his job, he would have to go back to work the Monday after Thanksgiving.

Roy was far from able but that Monday morning he went back to work. He taught algebra and advanced math classes and had done so for many years so preparation was not a problem. The noise and stress caused by having six different classes day after day was a definite problem. He often would stop at a bar for a drink after school. Soon he would have several drinks after school.

It was only after he was back in the classroom that his case came before a judge. Since he was back at his job, the judge awarded him nothing except having his medical bills paid and $1807.02. Roy never told Kate about going to the lawyer and Kate never saw any of the money.

Soon the time came when Roy would stay at the bar until the bartender called Kate to come and get him or he would have to call the police. Roy did not get mean. Instead, he would get weepy and sleepy. Lynn would go and pick him up most of the time. Kate would put him to bed. The next day, he would get up and go to school. After school he would head to the bar. Lynn or Kate would go and get him and take him home night after night.

Chapter 42

Without much planning, Lynn and two of his friends decided to go to California. Unfortunately, the semester at ASC still had a few weeks. Ignoring this fact, they packed up and went to California.

They went to work making cars for General Motors. One day one of the cars fell off the track. The workers all just backed up and watched the resulting chaos. New parts kept coming. Lynn went over and pulled the switch that stopped the assembly line before there was more damage. A crew came in and cleaned up the mess and after about an hour everyone went back to work. As Lynn left the plant on his way to the car, he was suddenly surrounded by four other workers.

They told him, "The next time something goes wrong with the assembly line, you just leave it alone. We would get the rest of the shift off with pay."

Lynn said, "What about the company we work for. They'll lose lots of money."

A worker said, "They don't care about us. Why should we care about them? They can afford it."

Another said, "Don't stop the belt if it happens again on our shift."

He went back to work. That was the only result of his stopping the line. Nothing more was said. He was quite happy with his job. His pay was good and he liked living in the Los Angeles area, there were a lot of different things to do on the weekends. Life was good.

About a month later, a part jumped the track again. Lynn started toward the lever. Suddenly, there was a guy on each side of him. He went back to his station. It was as they had said. The carnage was so great by the time the foreman had come and stopped the line that the men were sent home for the rest of the day.

Lynn was fuming. Right is right and wrong is wrong. He talked about quitting his job to his buddies. He had quite a bit of money saved up and so did the other two. They decided to stick it out for a few more months.

In Mesa, Kate was heartbroken. Now her son was gone also. It was hard but she knew that she and Roy were not nice to be around. Roy was sick physically and mentally, and she was sick emotionally. There was no joy in the household. So while she missed Lynn, she was glad, for his sake, that he was gone.

Then Roy got a long-distance phone call. His mother had fallen and broken her arm. She could no longer stay alone. Roy called his brother, Frank. Frank said, "Hire someone."

Roy called his sisters Mary and Florence. Susie would not let Florence bring her son Eddie around so Florence refused to go. Eddie had suffered from lack of oxygen in an accident and was a little slow mentally. Mary said that she was unable to go. That left it up to Roy and Kate to go to Colorado to take care of Susie. This time Kate drove the majority of the time. Since Susie could no longer stay alone, Roy took her to the doctor. The doctor ordered an ambulance and had her taken to the state home in Pueblo. Roy spent most of the next two days with her. It seemed as though it was an adequate facility. She had good meals and there was someone checking on her often during the day. As he left her and told her that he was going back home Susie said, "You promised that I would not be put into a home."

Roy heard the words over and over in his head as he went to pick up Kate. He had promised, but he just didn't see any other solution. He knew that he and Kate could not take her home with them and she would not have wanted to go anyway. She loved Colorado.

They were only home a week when Roy received a phone call. The nurse told him that he had to come back to Colorado. Roy was ill. He just did not see how he could go back. But this was his mother.

He went to Kate, "I need to go back to Colorado. I know I am not able to drive. I'm going to take the bus. I don't know how long I'll be gone."

Kate said, "Don't you want me to go with you?"

Roy said, "I just don't see how we can afford to have both of us go. I'll just go and sit with her and try to see what we can do to make things better for her. I'll come back as soon as I think I can."

Kate took him to the bus stop and watched with an aching heart as he went off to take care of his mother. Someone needed to be taking care of him. He was so disabled from the wreck. She went home. She was desolate. But she was angry, too. Roy's sisters and brothers had not had a terrible accident. Where were they?

Kate got a call a few days later. Susie had passed away. Roy was going to take care of the funeral and then he would be home.

Susie's other children came for the funeral. Roy had made arrangements. His brothers changed them. They bought a more expensive casket. They wanted a beautiful funeral. They didn't seem to understand that Susie and Lewis had no money. Roy went along with their wishes. He and Kate would pay for the funeral even though it took them several years.

Kate had no idea where Roy got the money for all the alcohol. Then she found out. After she would write checks, Roy would take the house payment out of the mailbox and tear up that check. Then he would draw that amount out of the account so that he had some money.

Kate didn't have a clue until she got a notice. She was told that if they wanted to keep the house, they would have to pay off the balance in full. There was no way for them to do that. They were given an eviction notice, so then they moved into an apartment. The wonderful house was gone. Kathleen was gone. The Roy she knew and loved was gone. Now there was a final blow. There was no apartment that would allow them to take Scaramouch. A neighbor took him, but the dog moped around, refused to eat, and died.

Lynn came back from California and moved into the apartment with them and still often picked Roy up at the bars but most of the time he was away doing other things. When he had brought Roy home and they had put him to bed, Lynn would say to Kate, "Mom, you've got to leave him. You can't do anything for him."

Kate said, "Where would I go? And besides, he's sick."

When the school year ended in June of 1960, Roy was told that he would not be rehired. Now they could office when the phone rang. There had been an accident with a semi truck that was loaded with the mushrooms that the pizza parlor used. If they would take the whole load, they could buy it at ten cents on the dollar. Lynn agreed to buy the semi truck load of mushrooms. He wondered what his boss would say. Fortunately, the boss was very pleased with Lynn's decision.

He was soon put in charge of the pizza parlor very close to ASC in Tempe. It had not made money since it went in. Lynn recognized the problem very soon. There were fights. There were people just sitting in the booths for long periods of time that were not spending money. After he had been there a few weeks, a very muscular, very big, black man came in,

Lynn went over to him, "Are you looking for a job?"

The man shook his head, "I just don't have the time. I need to study. I need to pass these classes."

Lynn said, "I'll pay you to study in that booth in the back. If I need you, which won't be very often, I'll tell you what to do,"

The man said, "I'll try it."

After that, when there was a fight, or Lynn wanted a group to move out, he would go and ask them to quiet down or leave. If they ignored him, he would go and tell his new employee, "Follow me."

The two of them would go back to the group that was misbehaving. They would look at Lynn's reinforcements and follow his directions.

Chapter 43

Roy and Kate were in California and Roy began his new job. He had never fully recovered from his accident but he figured he would do all right. Kate impressed upon him the fact that he could not drink alcohol on school nights, and he agreed. Kate got a job in a school cafeteria. They had been told that California school principals did not like to hire older people, so Roy got a toupee and Kate dyed her beautiful white hair blonde,

When Roy left, he drew out his Arizona retirement and bought himself a fairly new Cadillac. He had always wanted one so he decided he was going to have it. Kate knew it was a mistake, but decided it was a small price to pay to give Roy pleasure. So when they were fifty years old they basically started over. They had a fairly new car and were living in an apartment.

When Kate got off work, she called a real estate agent and started looking at houses. After much searching she found two houses that were fairly close to the school and she thought that they could afford to buy either one or the other. Then she had to convince Roy that they should buy one of them.

After a special supper of his favorite foods, she approached the subject, "Roy, I've found two houses that we can afford. Shall I make an appointment with the realtor on Saturday to look at them?"

Roy pushed himself away from the table and lit a cigarette. "I don't want to buy a house."

"It would be a good investment," Kate argued.

"I'm not going to buy another house," Roy said and went to his chair in the living room and read the newspaper.

They had decided that they did not need two cars. If Lynn came and picked up the older car, he could have it. When he arrived, he was with his girlfriend, Myra. Roy and Kate made arrangements for them to sleep in separate places. When you were in their house, you went by their rules. Then Roy came in and asked them if they wanted the big bed since he had found a marriage certificate. Myra was very irritated that Roy had gone through their things. It turned out that they had driven to Florence, Arizona where they were married by Lottie C. Divine, a Justice of the Peace, who was eighty-two years old, four foot nine, and humped over. She had given them a really nice little talk.

Roy did not drink on school nights but he did begin on Friday nights and Kate noticed a trend. Occasionally he would call in sick on Monday mornings. After much nagging by Kate, Roy agreed that he needed help. He could not quit drinking on his own, so his doctor gave him a pill to take. If he took any alcohol, he would become very ill and vomit it back up. It was a potent pill and Roy found he even had to change his shaving lotion. He cut out the alcohol and after a few difficult months he found he felt better without it.

During this time, Ann and Bill had moved to San Jose, and Bill began going to the University of Santa Clara to become a lawyer. Ann got a job with civil service and they lived on her wages. Their children, Pat and Erin, were going to a public school and doing fine. Money was short but they lived frugally and did all right. Bill finished law school and then he failed the bar exam.

Ann said, "That's it. You need to get a job. You can study nights,"

So that is what Bill did. The next time he took the exam he passed. Then they moved within a hundred miles of Kate and Roy. Bill went into real estate law, and Ann found a job as a computer processor.

Kate truly enjoyed having them so close. Life was beginning to improve. Then Lynn and Myra moved to the Los Angeles area and life was even better.

Roy taught and Kate worked in the school cafeteria. They made friends with Jesse and Alma, so for the first time in her life, Kate had a woman friend that was very special to her and to whom she was special as well. The four of them played bridge and went places together. Life was better than it had been in years.

Then one day Lynn called, "I know of a house that you two should buy. You're going to retire in a few years and you need a place of your own,"

Kate and Roy were in their sixties and she had to admit she was concerned about their prospects when they quit working. "I'll get your dad."

Lynn said, "Dad, I think you and Mom should look at this house as soon as possible. You have to make a decision quickly. It's going to sell soon,"

So that weekend, Lynn met them in the town of Yucaipa. He drove them up to a little house on Avenue A. It was a small, two bedroom, one bathroom house. It had a large, beautiful back yard. Kate held her breath. Roy said, "How much?"

Lynn told him, and Roy said, "We'll take it,"

It had been Myra's grandfather's house. He had obviously spent many hours in the back yard and it was very attractive. Since he had just died, the family wanted to get rid of the house quickly and settle the estate. Roy and Kate bought the house.

They were not going to retire for three years, so they had to rent the house. Their first renter was a young mother who would complain about the toilet clogging after she flushed diapers down it. They would call a plumber and pay the bill. After calling the plumber five times, Kate asked him why the toilet was always plugged up. When she found out it was from diapers, she let the mother know that from now on, she was responsible for the plumbing bill. She would not send the rent, so once a month they had to drive to Yucaipa to collect it. It was a relief when she moved out.

Then they rented the house to a young man. The check came every month and was always on time. That was the only time they heard from the renter. Life was sweet. Trips to Yucaipa were no longer necessary.

When Roy turned sixty-five years old, he needed to retire. It was time. He had never really recovered from the wreck and he and Kate were looking forward to moving into their little house. They sent a letter to the renter telling him that he and any housemates needed to move out because they were going to live in the house now.

The children and grandchildren all gathered for the big retirement party for Roy. Lynn and Myra put on a terrific spread. They had lots of delicious food and peach homemade ice cream. It was a wonderful party.

Over the years, Lynn and Myra had had the family over several times. They had a beautiful house that was kept spotless by the children and Myra. The food was always wonderfully cooked and there was lots of room for people to visit inside and out. Their children were capable and interesting grandchildren. Kate and Roy truly enjoyed the times at their house.

Then it was time to move. They gave up their apartment on the third floor in Pico Rivera and drove to their nice little house in Yucaipa. The 'wonderful' renters had not taken out the garbage farther than the garage or back yard for two years. The inside of the house was very dirty. The tears started rolling down Kate's cheeks. Fortunately, Bill and Ann were helping them move.

Bill consoled her. "It's going to be all right. Remember what it looked like just a few years ago. The damage is superficial. We're going to get it back like it was."

Kate knew he was right. She had never been afraid of hard work and that was all it would take. The work began immediately. They bought the largest yard sacks and began filling them. The garbage truck came and took some and left many more.

The next week when the garbage truck came, Roy and Kate were working in the front yard. Roy went over and asked, "Can't you take all these sacks? We are not done sacking up all the trash yet. If you take these we'll have more for you next week."

The man loading the bags said, "We're only allowed to take three bags a week. Sorry."

Three bags a week! They would have bags on their lawn for a year. They didn't know anyone with a truck so they could go to the dump and they didn't even know if there was a dump nearby.

"What can we do?" Roy asked,

The garbage collector suggested that Roy call the garbage company.

Kate phoned and the person she talked to suggested that they put a dumpster in the driveway. After the dumpster was delivered the hauling began in earnest. This was so much better. They would fill bags and throw them into the dumpster. When it was full, they would call the company and have it emptied and returned. Kate and Roy worked hard. Bill and Ann were over every weekend helping, but most of the work fell on Kate and Roy.

Chapter 44

The new house was a nice, little house on a nice street. Since they had moved to Yucaipa, Kate was looking forward to meeting her neighbors. Most of them were elderly ladies. The realtor had told her that many of them had lived in their houses for years. When she spoke to a neighbor, she was either ignored or the neighbor would respond and turn away. It was quite discouraging.

At this time, Kate made a decision. When they went to Yucaipa Baptist Church, she was going to go into the senior couples' Sunday school class. Her days of teaching Sunday school to the children were over.

Kate and Roy began working on their house with a vengeance. They cleaned off the old roofing. Finally, the dumpster was hauled away, and the excess garbage was gone. A hardware store delivered tar, tar paper, and roofing tiles. These things were delivered right on the roof of the house. Then more work began. Roy and Kate worked side by side. They smeared the tar and covered the roof with tar paper. Then they started at the bottom of the roof and began laying tiles. At the end of the day, they went in and ate sandwiches and took showers and went to bed. The next morning they were back at it. Finally, they were done. As they descended the ladder, Kate looked around. Oh, no, they weren't done! There was some of the old roofing still in the yard. So the next day was spent picking up and throwing away the old roofing. By working across the yard methodically, soon there was little evidence of the roofing project.

Kate really objected to the kitchen. She didn't mind that it was small because it was just the right size for her and Roy and it was easy to fix meals because she hardly had to move. She didn't like that it was so dark, though. One day she said to Roy, "I need a light over the sink."

So Roy worked on the new project. Soon there was a light over the sink. It helped a lot, but it was still too dark. Then she knew what to do. Her cousin, Obie Bontrager, came to visit. He helped Roy remove the top half of the wall that was between the kitchen and living room. She had them put a ledge about six inches wide and a post from the ledge to the ceiling. Then, where the door had been, she put in waist-high swinging, louvered doors. What a difference!

She had little storage in the kitchen. She did have a few cupboards for dishes and pans. She also had four drawers on top of each other that she liked very much. There was a small room for a washing machine off the kitchen and Roy put shelves above the machine. These could be used for storage. The laundry room also had a small pantry. Kate was beginning to like her new home a lot. It had a big back yard with a fig tree, an orange tree, a plum tree, and a gigantic English walnut tree. Myra's grandfather had had many plants growing on trellises in the back yard and it had been quite beautiful when they had bought the house. After the renters, it had become a neglected mess.

They painted the inside first and then they went to work on the outside. They worked side by side. They painted the outside yellow with white trim. When they had finished, they stood out by the street and looked at their little house. Now it looked better than it had when they had first looked at it.

Kate put roll-up blinds on the windows in the bedroom they would use. Then she bought lacy curtains to cover the blinds. In the living room she bought green drapes. They were usually open, so again she bought lacy curtains to help cut down the view into the house.

Slowly the neighbors began talking to them. It turned out that they had been disgusted with the renters. While the tenants were in the house, a toilet had been sitting on the front porch and one young man would dance around naked in the front yard shouting, "Hurry up, I need to use it," as the other young man would sit naked on the toilet. Of course, Kate and Roy had known nothing about their behavior, but between the stench of the garbage and the young men's outlandish behavior, the neighbors had been deeply offended.

As the neighbors began to accept Roy and Kate, they found that most of the people were elderly women, just as they had been told. Across the street two sisters lived together. They very much liked having a man around. They would call Roy over to make repairs. One of the sisters, Pansy, would come over and have a daily cigarette with Roy. They would bring him treats that he would then share with Kate after they left.

By the time they were done cleaning and painting it was too late to start a summer garden. Still, Kate had the large back yard to enjoy, and they would spend the evenings sitting in lawn chairs in the shade of the walnut tree.

One day they went to a nursery that had some baby chicks for sale. Kate bought a dozen of them. At night, they were kept in a big box. During the day, they would run around the back yard. Soon they were sleeping in an old shed out by the fence. How Kate enjoyed their antics while they were running around the yard. Then one day there was an egg. Soon there were plenty of eggs for her and Roy. It was fun to get fresh eggs for their breakfast.

One weekend Ann and Bill and Erin and Pat came over for the day. At that time, Erin had an Irish setter that she was training. Eventually, it would go for intense training and become a seeing-eye dog. For now, Erin's job was to teach it to follow the fundamental commands like 'sit' and 'heel.' Another aspect of its training was for the dog to learn to go out in public and not be distracted by what was going on around it.

At that point, however, the dog was not nearly as well trained as he would soon be, so when he saw the chickens, an entirely new experience, he started chasing them. How those chickens scattered! Of course, the more excited the chickens became, the more excited the dog became. Erin was trying to get him under control, but she was laughing so hard that the dog didn't think she was serious. When the fracas was over, the dog went over and sat down by Erin's feet. But where was the best laying hen? There was no sign of her. Finally, Kate said, "She must have flown over into Maude's yard. That's too bad. She gave me an egg every day without fail."

The rest of the chickens had gone into the little shed. The dog did not follow them into the shed. The rest of the visit was fine. Everyone had a good time. They ate and sat around and talked. Ann and Bill challenged Kate and Roy to a round of bridge. Pat and Erin climbed Flag Hill and entertained themselves. Erin played with the dog part of the time and both children liked to read. Soon after supper the family and the dog went back home.

The next day was Sunday and there was not one egg. They had plenty left over from other days so they had those for breakfast. Still, it was upsetting: who knew when they would start laying again? Besides, the hen that Kate knew would produce was gone.

Tuesday, Kate went into the garage. She heard a noise. There in the highest rafters was her egg-laying hen. She had been there for three days. Kate enticed it down with some chicken food and soon she was back to laying an egg a day.

Kate and Roy had begun eating the fryers as soon as they were four months old. Every few weeks, Roy would break a neck and Kate would douse the chicken up and down in boiling water. Then she would begin plucking feathers which she would then put into a paper bag and put into the garbage. As her group of chickens kept lessening and her garden plans began to grow larger, Kate realized she would need to put a fence around the garden to keep the chickens out. Actually, she would need to put up two fences, because she liked to throw the compost out into the yard, then bury it every so often, and then the next year plant her garden over the compost. Because she really liked her garden to be easily accessible, and because the chickens were in danger from roving cats and dogs, she decided that maybe she didn't want chickens after all. Also, she was not fond of all that feather plucking. So, slowly, one by one, the chickens were eaten. When the hen that laid an egg a day was left, she offered it to a man who lived down the hill and had many chickens.

The Yucaipa weather was wonderful for a garden, so the next year Kate started a garden where she had thrown her scraps for a year. Then everyday for a few hours, Kate would be out in the back yard working in the garden. She always had tomatoes, since they were a favorite of both Roy and Kate. She also planted corn, turnips, lettuce, squash, radishes, and carrots every year. She planted peanuts one year but the gophers got them. The plant would come up one day and then disappear the next.

Kate fought a constant battle with things that liked to eat her garden. It seemed as though the birds checked her yard, asking, 'Are they up yet?' and the bugs crawled along, asking, 'Are they up yet?'

The English walnut tree gave lots of nuts. One year they sat in the back yard and cracked nuts and put them in jars for gifts. Their plum tree gave them lots of plums even though it was hollow because of termites. Instead of ripening for Christmas as the navel oranges had at Palmers' so many years ago, the Valencia oranges were ready to eat in April.

The first year Kate and Roy planted a peach tree close to the clothesline. They waited impatiently for their freestone peaches for six years. Finally a few peaches were on the tree. Kate and Roy covered the tree with netting to protect the precious fruit from the birds. Daily, Kate examined the fruit, eager to pluck the first one when it was ripe. As the day approached, Roy began going out with her to look at the fruit to see if it was ready. Finally, the big day came. There were two plump peaches just begging to be eaten. They had their own little ceremony and each picked a peach. They went out to their chairs in the shade of the walnut tree. Kate watched and as Roy took a bite, so did she. She couldn't believe it. At first she was surprised and then she was angry. It was a cling peach! She had paid a premium price for a freestone peach tree six years ago. It was just too hard to can cling peaches, and if the tree was any good there would be plenty of peaches to can. So that season they ate cling peaches and gave away what they couldn't eat. When the season was over, Kate went out with a handsaw and cut that tree off about eight inches above the ground. The next year she bought another freestone peach tree. This one she planted way out in the back of her big yard.

They did not plant an apple tree because one of their favorite outings was going up to famous Oak Glen and buying apples. A trip to the orchard usually resulted in a lunch at one of the restaurants and sometimes they would walk through the shops, or at least Kate would. Roy had arthritis in his feet and he really hated to walk very much because it was so painful. Still, he never minded sitting on one of the benches, having a cigarette or two, and visiting with other smokers while he waited for Kate.

Kate considered the garden hers, so she went out with powder for the greedy bugs. Then she would put netting over her plants to protect them from the birds and also to protect the birds from eating the poisoned bugs. She had an on-going feud with the gophers. She put out poison and traps, and she thought that they helped some. She had cabbages come up in a prolific manner, but soon she found holes in many of the cabbages. Then she noticed that the cabbages were being eaten but the other plants were not. Since the uninvited guests seemed to prefer the cabbages to other things, she just left them alone. She planted cabbage each year. She and Roy had plenty of cabbage to eat and it was nice that the little destroyers seemed to stick to the cabbages and leave her other plants alone.

Chapter 45

Their children all seemed to be doing fine. Herb and Billie had two daughters, Katherine and Julia. He had bought a barbershop in Flagstaff and she had finally gotten a job teaching first grade in the Flagstaff public schools. She had taught third grade in Tuba City one year before she was hired as a first-grade teacher in Flagstaff. Their two girls seemed happy and all was well with them.

Ann and Bill and their two children, Pat and Erin, were now living in California. They would come to visit quite often. Bill had his law degree and Ann was working with computers.

Lynn and Myra were also living in California. They had a beautiful house in Colton with over an acre of land. They now had a total of nine children; Kelly, Kasey, Lance, Clinton, Keegan, Laren, Calyn, Kameron, and Kerry. Often a few children at a time would come and spend time with Roy and Kate. Those times were always special.

Frank had only been working in Prescott to earn money to buy a farm in South Dakota. So he and Elizabeth had moved to South Dakota. Elizabeth had never been fond of farm life but she grew accustomed to it. She did get a teaching job which helped them to have ready cash each month. Elizabeth and

Frank had five children; John, Matthew, Bob, Jeff, and Susan.

Roy and Kate were quite pleased with their children and their families.

Chapter 46

Roy watched lots of sports on television, so he got in the habit of entering the contests to guess the final points. He would put Kate's name on the form and send it in. She won quite often and became known as a sports expert. When asked questions about sports, she would just smile.

Billie and Herb's daughter, Julie spent her senior year with her grandma and grandpa. She had a falling out with her dad because she became pregnant by a black man named Marvin and, even though she lost the baby, she would not break up with him. At the time, Marvin did not marry Julie, and she was planning to quit school and find a job. She only had part of her senior year to finish high school, so Billie sent her to live with her grandma and grandpa so that she could get a high school diploma,

In many ways it was a difficult year. Julie was angry about the fact that control of her life was taken out of her hands. She did not help with the housework unless forced. After all, it was not her decision to come here. Kate found it was easier to do the work herself rather than to fight with Julie about it.

Roy and Kate had forgotten how different it was with another person in the house. They had been taking it easy after all their hard work of cleaning and remodeling. Now there was an angry teenager in the house. School had always been hard for Julie and it was still hard. Roy helped her with her homework every evening. The goal was for her to graduate from high school. Everyone breathed a sigh of relief when she graduated and Billie came to take her back to Flagstaff.

When Billie came to get Julie, she presented her folks with a puff quilt that she had made. She had asked every grandchild, child and their spouses to use liquid embroidery to make a picture on a six-inch square and then send it back to her. While Julie was in Yucaipa, Billie had sewed two squares together , then stuffed them with polyester, and then sewed the squares together. It was quite nice but not very practical. It was much too heavy to sleep under.

Because of all the conflict between them, Herb had broken off all relations with Julie. Once again she became pregnant with Marvin's baby and now she was on her own. She got a job working in an apartment. She cleaned and cooked and babysat for two other women. Billie was furious with Marvin for not taking care of her; he was five years older than she was; he had a job with Purina, and she thought Julie should be married and cooking and cleaning for Marvin. They did get married before their son, Maximillian, was born. Marvin bought a lot with a house trailer on it, and that is where they lived.

Chapter 47

Roy took up woodworking. He made bowls and then eventually began to make a wooden storage for each of his children and grandchildren. He was working in the garage every afternoon, so Kate began quilting in the afternoons. As each new grandchild or great grandchild was born, he or she would be presented with a wonderful, small grandma-made quilt. How her family loved the quilter and cherished the quilts. It was quite comfortable for Roy in the garage and his working in there kept the small living room neat and clean.

Lynn's daughter, Kasey saw the quilt in progress and said, "Oh, Grandma, I wish you would make a quilt for me now that I'm grown. How I would love to have one of your quilts."

So now Kate began making larger quilts to give away. She gave one to Kasey and then to Kelly. One day Billie said, "How come you're making quilts for Lynn's girls and not mine?"

Kate said, "They asked for one."

Billie said, "That's not fair. You raised us not to ask for things. We are to be satisfied with what we have."

That night she called Kathy and Julie and said, "If you want your Grandma Kate to make you a quilt, you had better write her a letter and tell her so."

They did write the letters and after that Kate always had a big quilt in the quilting frame in the garage. She would work out there much longer than Roy.

After living in the neighborhood all this time, Kate got where she recognized the neighborhood children and would often have conversations with them as they played or walked on the street. Because their lawn was so open and so nice, soon the children would play on the lawn. Kate enjoyed them.

One day as Billie and Herb were leaving Kate's to go back to Flagstaff, Billie said to her Mom, "Remember when Elizabeth started dating and you crocheted a bedspread. Where is it? And what are you going to do with it?"

Kate took her into her bedroom and took a crocheted bedspread out of her trunk.

When Billie looked at it, she said, "This isn't the way I remember it at all. I thought it was a lighter color."

Kate said, "I made two. The other one is down in a consignment shop. I have it for sale for eighty dollars."

Billie was quite agitated. "I'll give you the eighty dollars. I really want that bedspread. But we have to go home before the consignment shop opens. Please go and pick it up and the next time we come I will give you the money."

Kate said, "You don't have to pay me. I thought no one wanted it,"

"I bet Elizabeth would love to have this one," Billie stated.

The second Thanksgiving in Yucaipa, Kate and Roy started a tradition which they continued up into their late eighties. They invited their children and their families over for dinner. The corn, lettuce, cucumbers, carrots, radishes, tomatoes, and onions all came from Kate's garden. She would have apple butter that she made. She made lots of preserves but found that the apple butter was the one most often preferred. However, she always had takers for her other fruit preserves, too.

Lynn and Myra and their children came, and Ann, Bill, Pat, and Erin came. Both families always brought something. Sometimes Billie and Herb drove over from Flagstaff in their motor home.

Ann would bring different salads. Her dishes were often unique. One year the bowl was a huge hollowed out squash. She liked bringing combinations that were not common. Everyone looked forward to her dishes.

Since Roy and Kate moved into the Yucaipa house just as their oldest grandchildren turned twenty, soon great grandchildren were coming to the dinners also. Kasey married Christopher Cahan and little Alexander was the first great grandchild to come. The house was small but Kate would make the table out of boards on sawhorses. She bought a long white piece of cloth that covered both of the eight foot boards, and she hemmed both ends. Then she bought a long red piece of lace that was seventeen feet long and covered the white. It was quite beautiful. Kate really liked everyone sitting at the same table. As soon as the meal was over most people moved into the beautiful backyard. Lynn didn't. He nearly always took a thirty minute nap after eating. Kate usually needed a power nap also, but hers were only about ten minutes.

One week before Thanksgiving, Kate had filled out a raffle slip at many stores, and that year she won her turkey. After that, every year, she and Roy would go to every store and fill out slips to win a turkey. For the next several years the turkey Kate cooked was one she had won. Often the proprietor of the shop where she was depositing a slip would say, "If you win, I want a piece of that turkey." Without fail, either on Thanksgiving day if the store was open, or else the day after Thanksgiving, Kate would take a complete turkey dinner on a nice sturdy paper plate to the worker in the store where she had won the turkey.

Kate was ahead of her time as far as recycling and watching the country's resources. She and Roy shared the newspaper with their neighbor. Harriet would get the paper, read it and keep the television schedule. Then she would fold it just like new and pass it on to them. They split the cost of the paper.

Kate did have an automatic washing machine which her children had bought for her. She had no desire to have a dryer because she loved the freshness of the way the clothes smelled after they had hung on the line to dry. She did eventually buy a small electric dryer that she put into the garage and used only in an emergency or when she needed to wash on a rainy day.

She recycled all her garbage into her garden. She knew that this was one of the best fertilizers and it cost nothing except a little effort. She would put her compost in one area of her yard all year long. She would turn the dirt with a shovel to bury the compost along with the odor. The next year that would be her garden plot. One year Roy put a mattress over part of the garbage and raised earthworms for fishing and for the garden. Each year the gophers and crows kept Roy and Kate busy defending their garden. One year when the crows were especially numerous, Roy took a .22 rifle and shot a crow. It tumbled down to the ground. Roy spread the wings of the dead crow out on the yard, right next to the garden, and then he went into the house.

That evening, as Kate was cleaning the kitchen, Roy walked out into the back yard. He heard a strange, rustling sound and looked up. There were many crows flying in circles over his head. He had taken a few steps into the yard, when suddenly the crows started flying straight at him. He ran to the house, hurried inside, and slammed the door. He and Kate stood and looked at the crows flying around outside the door. They were astounded. Needless to say, they did not go into the back yard as they usually did for the rest of the day.

The next morning, Kate cautiously opened the back door and looked out. There was not a crow is sight. They were not bothered with crows again for the next two years. When they returned, Roy did not have the nerve to shoot another crow. Nor did he find it necessary. They never again bothered the garden as much as before he had shot the crow.

Nearly every year, Kate and Roy would go to South Dakota to see Elizabeth and her family. They knew how difficult it was to get away when you had cows to milk and animals to care for, along with the daily chores that had to be done without fail. Also, Kate enjoyed being back on a farm. She especially loved the smell. One of her favorite days was the day Elizabeth decreed that the corn was ready for picking. How Kate and Liz picked! Then they took off the husks and cleaned off the silk. Kate liked every bit of it except cleaning off the silk, but her mother would not have dreamed of leaving one strand of silk and she was the one who had taught Kate.

That night, supper consisted of corn on the cob and bread and lots of butter. The men came in after working in the fields all day so they were quite hungry and would eat several ears of corn each. This was a custom followed each year when the first crop of corn was picked and everyone in the family looked forward to it.

Roy and Kate enjoyed being with Elizabeth's family but they also enjoyed the trips to get there. Over the years they went through Yellowstone National Park, Mount Rushmore, Wall Drug, Bryce Canyon, Zion National Park, and every other picturesque place between Yucaipa and South Dakota.

They would usually stop at Billie's in Flagstaff either coming or going. They would also visit the Colorado people; Kate's sister Lena and her brothers, Mose and Perry and their families. Sometimes they would head north and go through Idaho and visit Roy's brothers, Frank and Don, and his sisters, Mary and Florence, and their families.

Chapter 48

One year for Christmas, Billie and Herb decided to take everyone deep sea fishing instead of buying presents. Billie called Pat, who lived in San Diego, and asked him to set it up. At that time, as many people as could squeeze in the boat could go for $450 and eat free all day long. Alcoholic drinks were extra but cokes, coffee, sandwiches, and chips were included in the price. Pat and Bill often went deep sea fishing, so Pat knew just who to call.

The smallest person along was Kathy and David's second son, Nathaniel. He was only a few months old, so he was carried in a stomach pack by Kathy or David. Jeremy, on the other hand, was an active three-year-old. Kathy attached a leash to him so that he would have freedom but could be kept from falling overboard. The oldest person along was Herb's mother, Ida. Kate and Roy were almost as old. Ida did not fish but she did enjoy seeing the seals and looking down at the fish and the beautiful ocean.

Each person had a gunny sack. As a fish was caught, it would be put into that person's sack. Eight-year-old Calyn caught a fish almost as large as he was, but the most successful person was Ann. While she was reeling in a twelve-inch fish, a larger fish came and swallowed her fish. She was quite excited and was reeling as fast as she could when suddenly another even larger fish came and swallowed the second fish. So as the net was lowered over the side, Ann brought in three fish at one time.

As they started back after a day of fishing, the crew of the boat started filleting the fish. They cut off and kept the beautiful large pieces of fish, but the scraps they threw back into the water. Soon the ocean was alive with seagulls, diving for the scraps of fish thrown back into the sea.

It was a beautiful day. Kathy and her family of four had spent the days before the boat trip with David's family in a hotel in San Diego. His Gee grandparents had rented several rooms so that the family could all meet and be together. They had had a lovely time with his parents, grandparents, and brothers and sister.

The fishing trip was the culmination of the holidays and everyone had to head back to their homes and work. The other Gees had gone their various ways on the morning of the fishing trip. Kathy and David and the boys were flying out of Phoenix early the next morning. Herb and Billie were giving them a ride from San Diego to the Phoenix Airport. Herb was driving along the desert road between the state line and Phoenix. Billie was trying to stay awake to keep him company when David sat up from where he had been resting and asked, "Where are we?"

Herb answered, "We'll be in Phoenix in about an hour."

David said, "I need to call home. When you see a place that might have a phone, pull in so I can call home."

Herb said, "Can't you just call from the airport? We'll be there soon,"

But David insisted, "I need to call as soon as possible."

Soon after that they came to a small service station. David called his parents' house. His dad had been trying to reach him to tell him that his mother had committed suicide. So David and Kathy went back to Flagstaff instead of Virginia.

Mary Ellen Gee had been an exceptional parent. Her children knew that they could do anything. She was a loving, imaginative, caring individual who drove herself to do more than most people would have even considered. She had run a preschool and taught those little ones to have self-worth. She would sew far into the nights. She had many handmade things around the house. She was a much better than average painter. How sad that her own grandchildren would not have the benefit of her love and affection.

Chapter 49

Kate and Roy enjoyed having Lynn and Ann and their families around. Ann and her family would visit quite often. Lynn was a workaholic. He would come out to visit on special days, birthdays and holidays. He would call frequently, but he worked long hours and often seven days a week. He did usually have a garden that he would tend and he and Kate would compete in a friendly matter. Who had the largest, reddest, most tomatoes? Who had the biggest pumpkin, most peas, or tallest corn?

In 1979 there was a tornado in South Dakota. Elizabeth's married son, John, was in a silo when the tornado struck and the silo collapsed, and John was killed. He had married a fine young woman, Joyce, and had a son whom they had named Jason.

Lynn and Myra made arrangements so that Roy and Kate could go to Elizabeth at this time. They bought the plane tickets and made sure they got to the airport. John was their oldest grandson but he was only in his low twenties. It was a terrible tragedy.

Chapter 50

Kate and Roy had been married for fifty years. All their children were coming and many of their grandchildren. Lynn and Myra and Ann and Bill had rented a hall and had invited all the guests. They sent out invitations, cooked the food, and handled everything. These two couples put out all the expense of the party.

The party was to be on Saturday. Herb and Billie came on Thursday. Elizabeth and Frank got in on Friday. Kate got up Friday morning and began to try to lift the very heavy gifts that Herb and Billie had brought. Whatever could they be? About two in the afternoon, Kate said, "It couldn't be gold. It would be worth a fortune if it was gold and weighed that much,"

Billie went to Herb and said, "If Mom sleeps on it another night, she'll know exactly what it is. She had this uncanny knack for figuring out what a gift is."

Billie told Herb the following story of the washing machine from when she was a child:

"Mom loved to know what was in a package before she opened it. When Dad had ordered her first automatic washing machine and was walking around very pleased with himself, Mom was stumped. She knew he had bought her something nice, but she couldn't find a package. She'd asked questions of all of us but we kept mum. But she kept asking and finally in exasperation I said, 'He bought you a new white dress. Now you won't be surprised.'

Mom said, 'Oh, goody, I'm getting my new washing machine.'

I was flabbergasted. How did she interpret a white dress as a washing machine?"

Billie concluded "We better have her open the packages tonight."

Billie had been working hard on the folks' fiftieth anniversary present. She'd been collecting pennies and put one for each day they were married into glass jars like the old fashioned kind that stores had kept candy in to sell. The jars were different sizes from a quart up to a gallon. The gallon ones held about five thousand pennies and were very heavy. How Kate laughed when she opened the gifts and found the pennies. At least once, Billie had surprised her.

Billie had also collected miniatures that reminded her of her childhood, and she had wrapped each one individually. She also bought a shadow box to put each item in to form a display. There was a hand ice cream freezer, a Willy's jeepster, a rifle, and a deer. There were many farm animals. There was a sewing machine, a bookcase, and a piano. There were many more items that brought back wonderful memories. As each box was opened, it would remind someone there of a happy time.

Elizabeth and Frank bought them a beautiful vase that said 'fifty years' in gold. Inside they had put fifty fifty-cent pieces.

Her granddaughter, Kathy, had made her a family tree and had it framed. The grandparents' names were on the roots. Roy and Kate's names were on the trunk of the tree. Their children and their spouses' names were on the branches. The grandchildren and great grandchildren's names were on the leaves.

Roy gave Kate a bell. If she wanted a cup of coffee, all she had to do was ring the bell. Occasionally, she would ring the bell in the morning, if he was up before her. She did love to lie in bed and drink her first cup of coffee. Most mornings, Kate was up before Roy. He had always made the coffee before he went to bed in the wee hours of the morning, and she just didn't have the heart to wake him to get her coffee. During the day, she would often wait on herself. Old habits die hard.

A few weeks after the party, Roy called his brother, Frank. There had been hard feelings when their mother had died. Roy had had to go to Colorado and take care of the funeral even though he was not physically able. It was way too close to his accident. Words had been said, and Roy decided that it was time to heal those wounds. So, Kate, Roy, Frank and his wife, Mary, went to New Orleans together and had a wonderful week. People had given money at the anniversary party so they had enough to go and keep up financially with his rich brother, Frank.

Chapter 51

Erin, Ann's daughter, had married Jeff Doran. They had met when Mount St. Helen had erupted and they worked with dogs finding bodies. Jeff worked out in the field with the dogs. Erin worked at the base manning the radio. While he worked, Jeff took pictures and wrote about what was happening. He had the book printed. *Search on Mount St. Helen* was very informative, the photography was outstanding, and it was easy to read. After they were married, Erin and Jeff had a daughter named Jamie Lynn. Ann and Bill went to Seattle to spend time with their daughter and first grandchild.

As for Lynn and Myra, they had a rocky marriage. One day Myra was complaining about him to her friend, Gayanne.

Gayanne replied, "He doesn't seem so bad to me. He sure works hard,"

A few days later, Myra began throwing Lynn's things out onto the lawn in front of the house. She called Gayanne and said, "You think Lynn is so great, you just come and get him."

Gayanne was surprised. She and Lynn had talked very little to each other, but she thought maybe Myra had misunderstood their few conversations. She went out to try to talk to Myra, but Myra wouldn't listen, so Gayanne collected Lynn, who had since come home, and his things and took him away from there. They did eventually get married.

Kate had always believed that marriage was for better or for worse, so she was concerned because Lynn and Myra were breaking up after so many years and so many children together. But she had to admit that Gayanne was good for Lynn. He was happier than he had been for years, and sometimes they would do fun things as well as just work. Kate also had to admit she loved Gayanne. She was a happy, positive person that treated her son very well. Kate had always loved Ann's husband, Bill, and now she loved Gayanne also.

Gayanne had three sons still at home; Tim, K. C., and Kelly. Her daughter, Lynda, was married but lived close enough so that they could visit. Lynda had a son, Brandon. Lynn and Myra's children hadn't yet started having children of their own so Brandon made Lynn an instant grandpa.

Ann's son, Patrick Michael, married Sherrie Hoffa and they both were working to get their doctor's degrees. They did get their degrees in 1985. They both went into research. Sherrie went into the private factor and would eventually make quite a name for herself and have a lucrative income. Pat went into research at the university. He would write grants to finance his research. Then in 1986, Sherrie was going to have a baby. Pat was very pleased. He could hardly wait. Ann and Bill were looking forward to the coming baby.

The last Friday morning in February of the following year, Bill called Kate and Roy. Ann had passed away during the night. Kate had known for years that Ann was in lots of pain. Bill and Ann had bought themselves a waterbed to help relieve her back. She had also bought a machine that hung her upside down by her ankles to help with her backaches. But even with all her pain, she never missed work. Just the weekend before, Ann and Kate had enjoyed a day of shopping and visiting together.

Ann had stopped at a doctor's office on her way home from work that Friday. She was having chest pains and coughing spells and had trouble breathing. She had tried over the counter cough medicine to no avail. She was hoping for something more powerful. The doctor gave her a prescription and told her to sleep and rest until Monday. She had a bronchial infection.

She had bought a contour lounger that she sat in when she had trouble sleeping. Because of the coughing, that was where she headed when she got home. The medicine must have helped because she immediately went to sleep. She was there when Bill came home from work. She was still there when Bill was ready to go to bed about 10:00.

Bill woke her and said, "Don't you want to go to bed?"

Ann answered. "No, I'm going to stay here."

About midnight, Bill went in to check on her. She was no longer alive. He could not feel a pulse and she was very cold. He knew she had been dead for a little while. He called 911. The ambulance came and the EMTs tried to revive her, but she was gone and there was no hope. The EMTs told Bill they were required to always try to revive the person. They took her away.

The next morning a police detective came to talk to Bill. Because Bill did not know that Ann had gone to the doctor, there was no prior indication that she had been sick. They told him that they had a court order to perform an autopsy and Bill was not to leave town.

Bill knew he was in no way responsible, but he did feel a little uncomfortable. It was not pleasant to have the police treat him as a suspect in the death of his beloved Ann.

The autopsy showed that she had a seriously enlarged heart. It was a wonder that she had not been bedridden. She and Bill had talked about what to do in case of either of their deaths, so he had her cremated and scattered her ashes over the ocean from a small plane.

It was typical of Ann not to want a fuss made over her, but there was no closure for the rest of the family. Roy looked gray. The life had gone out of him. The family gathered but no one knew what to do.

Pat and Sherrie had Christopher David less than a month later. What should have been a joyous occasion was bittersweet. Ann would have made a wonderful grandmother. She shared an attribute with her dad; Ann and Roy were the least judgmental people in the world. They seemed to realize that they had not 'walked in other people's shoes' so they were seldom critical of choices that people made. They saw the good in people and ignored the bad.

Sherrie's mother, Darlene, was a loving and proud grandmother. She took care of Christopher when Sherrie and Pat were working. They did, eventually, hire a nanny and light housekeeper. Bill and Jack, Sherrie's dad, enjoyed their roles as grandpas.

On Ann's birthday the following June, Pat had a get-together for the family. Everyone gathered at Bill's house. Pat had collected stories about Ann and put them together into a book. Everyone who was there was given a copy of *Amazing Ann*. They read the stories and talked about what a good parent, sister, daughter, and friend Ann had been.

Chapter 52

In 1989, Lynn once again took charge and had a party for his mom's 80th birthday. He and Gayanne made arrangements at a fine restaurant. They invited family and friends. Billie and Kathy wrote a poem and had people send letters of stories about Kate. The letters came to Billie's house and she compiled them into a book, which she gave to Kate at the party.

Lynn had needle pointed a poem and presented it to her;

The test of life thru eighty years
Through all the joy and all the tears
You stood with love and faithful heart
Through some loved ones too soon did part
Mother, Sister, Friend and Wife
You stayed on course throughout your life
And as the tempest turns to dawn
I thank the Lord you are my Mom
Love, Lynn 10-16-89

The following year was Roy's eightieth birthday. Billie and Kathy again sent out a poem about Roy. Billie had so looked forward to the mail when she was getting letters for Kate's birthday that she decided to have his letters go directly to him so he could look forward to it as she had. For the month before his birthday, getting the mail was a great experience. He got letters from former students whose lives he had touched. He got letters from nephews, nieces, grandchildren, children and friends. Unfortunately, he did not think to keep the letters and place them in a book as Billie had done for Kate.

When they had been married sixty years, getting mail was again a great experience because many people sent them congratulations. How nice to hear from so many people. Roy went all out. On the night of their anniversary, he took Kate for a ride in a carriage behind two large, beautiful white horses. They ended up at a steak house where they had dinner with Gayanne and Lynn.

Chapter 53

Soon after the wonderful weekend when they had celebrated their sixtieth wedding anniversary, Kate had a terrible experience. One minute she was driving home after grocery shopping. The next instant, her vision was garbled. She could see out of the side of her eyes if she turned her head, but not very well. Looking straight ahead everything was blotted out. She was close to home, so she slowly drove up Avenue A and into her driveway.

She could no longer read. She could no longer quilt. She could no longer drive. She went to several doctors. They told her that macular degeneration was the leading cause of blindness in senior citizens, and there was no cure. She had never heard of it before. For the first six weeks she was incapacitated. She would still go sit in her back yard, but she did very little.

Then one day, she said to herself, 'Enough!' She had heard of Dial-a-Ride that would pick up senior citizens that could not or would not drive. Roy could still drive, but she liked to go much more than he did. She memorized the number so she could call for a ride when she wanted to go somewhere.

Billie bought her the Bible on tape, so every day she could listen to the Bible. Then Pat and Sherrie came over. They called the Braille Institute and had them send her a tape player and books on tape. She enjoyed that much more than television. With television, she could sort of see the screen if she turned her head and looked out of the corner of her eye, but the picture was distorted. She watched a few quiz shows with Roy every day, but when he watched sports, she would listen to books on tape.

Roy's hands were very arthritic, but he took over writing the checks to pay the bills. She could put the return addresses and the stamps on the envelopes. She would put them out for the mail person to pick it up.

Chapter 54

Soon after Kate had lost her sight, Billie and Herb found that on their way back home from their lot in San Felipe, Baja California they were within five hours of her parents' house. They decided to go by and see them and then go on to Flagstaff the next day.

When they got to Yucaipa, Roy and Kate's house was deserted. Billie and Herb thought they had gone grocery shopping or out to lunch. So they stayed in the motor home for a couple of hours. When they didn't show up, Billie went back to talk to their neighbor, Harriet.

She told them, "Lynn and his wife came by and they all went to Stateline, Nevada."

So off Billie and Herb went. When they got to Stateline, it had only two big casinos. So they went walking through them. Billie found Kate at a nickel machine. She had a cupful of nickels.

"It looks like you are doing well," Billie said.

"I am," Kate replied. "I just seem to keep winning."

They talked for quite a while about the weather, about how long they were staying, and about the food. Then Billie said, "Do you know where Lynn is?"

Kate stopped pulling the arm on the one-armed-bandit. "Do you know Lynn?"

"I'm Billie. I didn't know you didn't recognize me."

"Oh, Billie, I just thought you were someone friendly."

Roy and Gayanne couldn't stop gambling to visit. They went to Stateline to play poker. Gayanne always said, "I like taking Roy and getting into a game with players that don't know us. They always think, 'an old man and a broad, I've got it made.' We always win a few hands before they realize that we know how to play poker."

Gayanne was called 'Poker Mama' and Roy was given a name also, though Gayanne couldn't remember later what it was. The dealers knew that they were quite capable players.

Chapter 55

One time, Bill and Ann had gone to a party in another town. While staying in the town, they made arrangements to stay at the motel closest to where the party was. Driving back to their motel, Bill had gotten a ticket for drunk driving. Ann was so angry about it that she had been arrested for disorderly conduct. After they paid the fines, they bought a van with a bed and a bathroom. That way, when they were done partying, they would go out in the van and go to bed without having to drive anywhere.

After Ann's death, Bill tried working eighty hour weeks but that didn't help the loneliness. When he realized work wasn't going to cure him, Bill took the van and traveled around. He went to the tip of Baja California, but he also traveled to many places in the United States. including Nashville, Tennessee. He would stop early in RV parks and sit at a table and wait for someone to walk past. He would then invite them to stop for a drink and a visit. He found that people would tell him the most intimate, interesting and private things. He guessed it was because they planned never to see him again.

Ann had tried to get him to invest quite a bit of money in computer companies in the stock market. He had said, "No way." That was a mistake. Ann had periodically invested a much smaller amount and he found that he had well over a million dollars worth of stock.

Bill had a chance to buy a condo on the beach. He was assured that he could keep it rented for $1500 a week. He had a real estate agent that helped him but she wanted a personal relationship and he did not.

Kate and Roy were bereft. Bill and Ann had been over often. Ann would plan outings with Kate. Bill would be deep sea fishing or he and Roy enjoyed the sports on television. Now Ann was gone. It was such a lonely time.

Fortunately, when Bill was in California, he continued to call Kate and Roy and spend afternoons with them. He collected his change and gave it to them for Christmas one year. Kate used it to refurnish her old trunk. He would stop by whenever he was fairly close and visit with them and take them out to dinner. Sometimes Kate would make them toast and white gravy.

Bill found that he really enjoyed going down to Rosarita Beach in Mexico. He put a small trailer in a park and spent several days each month down there. The people in the park were friendly and helped one another. He planned to write a book about lawyers but it never seemed to get done.

He and Lynn became better friends than they had ever been and Lynn quite often went down to Rosarita Beach and stayed with him for a day or two,

Unfortunately, the bottom fell out of the real estate market while he was away from home. He still sold the house that he and Ann had lived in for a nice profit. Had he sold it six months earlier, he would have made a much larger profit. His partner bought his share of the partnership. They tried to sell the building that their law office was in since his partner planned to downscale. The city gave them difficulties. So again, Bill did not make as much as he expected.

Bill found that he was happiest in Mexico in the little trailer park. He did go to San Felipe while Herb and Billie were there on the lot they had won through the contest of the National Pen Company. Bill loved the Pacific Ocean side of Baja. The weather was much better. It was not nearly as hot in the summertime. The area was more built up. He said that San Felipe was still having growing pains.

One weekend Bill had put his flag up his flagpole in the trailer park. This was the way he invited people in to watch his television. Bill had a satellite dish and could get many stations. Several friends came over to watch a soccer game on his TV. When the game was over, one of his cronies went over to wake him up and he was dead.

They called a doctor and his son, Pat, who lived in San Diego. Pat called Erin and she flew down from Washington. The authorities did not want them to transport the body back to the United States, but they did not object to a cremation and disposing of the ashes in the ocean. So that is what Erin and Pat did.

Later, Pat had a get-together for Bill as he had for Ann. Everyone gathered at his house in San Diego. Afterwards, Lynn wanted to go to the trailer park in Rosarita Beach. Kate had always intended to go down with Bill, so when Billie and Herb decided to take their motor home, she and Roy decided to go along.

The people in the park accepted them as Bill's family. They sat around the park campfire and talked about the good times. The power went out on the beach and in the park, so Herb fired up the generator and kept the bunch that weren't drinking alcohol in coffee. It was a nice time. But Roy and Kate were exhausted. As soon as breakfast was over the next morning they headed back to Yucaipa.

Chapter 56

Christmas was coming. It was going to be great. Kate's granddaughter, Kathy, and her family were coming from Oconomowoc, Wisconsin. Billie and Herb were coming from Flagstaff. It would be wonderful to have a houseful. Kate cleaned house and then suddenly realized that she was worn out. She dragged herself to bed. Oh, how she hoped she wouldn't be too tired when her family was visiting.

Roy seemed happy that they were coming, too. But he didn't exert himself like Kate did. She wanted everything to be perfect. At times like this her house was pretty small but most of the time it was a very nice size.

The 24th of December arrived. It was fun. The children didn't mind sleeping on the floor or couch in the living room, and she had the extra bedroom for Kathy and David. Herb never left home for the night without his motor home so of course they had a place to sleep. They offered to put Keegan or the two boys up on the couch in the motor home but Jeremy and Nathaniel both said, "No, we'll just sleep on the floor in the living room. Keegan can have the couch."

Kate smiled as the children opened presents the next morning. It was so exciting to have youngsters around. Kathy and David gave each child fifty dollars so they would have money on the rest of the trip. They were going by train from Los Angeles to San Diego and going to Sea World. They would also have dinner with Pat, Sherrie and Christopher one night. They were also going to Disneyland. They would also go to David's Grandma Gee's home one day. So on the morning of the 26th they were on their way to their next destination. Billie and Herb went home on the 27th.

Kate and Roy let out a sigh of relief. It had been wonderful but they were both quite worn out. It seemed that two days of excitement meant three days of resting, but it was worth it. They spent the rest of the year resting. The new year of 1997 came in and then Kate realized that she and Roy were not eating. They both drank coffee but food just sat on their plates. Kate would fix them each a piece of toast which was their usual breakfast, hers with apple butter or jam. Roy's had lots of butter. The toast would eventually be thrown away.

One night Billie called to see how things were going,

Kate answered the phone, "Hello."

Billie said, "I called to see how you two are doing"

Kate said, "I'm sick. I'm really sick.'

Billie asked, "Are you throwing up?"

"No."

"Do you have a fever?"

"No. I don't think so. I'm just so weak. Your Dad and I are not eating."

Billie was concerned, "Do you need someone to get you some soup or something? Have you been to the doctor? Do I need to get a hold of someone to help you?"

"No, it can't be the flu. We've had our flu shots. We just need to rest and get some sleep. I'm going to bed now." And Kate hung up the phone,

She had answered the phone in the living room and was on her way to bed. As she walked by Roy's chair, he stuck his hand out and stopped her, "I killed our Kathleen. I hit her head with a branch and I killed her."

Kate was dumbfounded. "No you didn't. She had a brain tumor." She wasn't sure she would make it to bed, so she just kept going. As she staggered into the bedroom she thought, 'We have to discuss this tomorrow, but I just can't tonight.' Didn't Roy know that Kathleen had been troubled with that vagueness? Maybe not. It was my job to take care of the children. Maybe I had never told him. I'll tell him about it tomorrow but I have to go to bed right now.

The next morning, Kate dragged herself out of bed. Roy was already up. It was drizzling outside. Roy said, "I need cigarettes. Will you go with me to get them?"

Kate knew she made it much easier when she went with him. He would drop her off at the door and wait, with the motor running, while she went in and bought the cigarettes. That way he did not have to park and go in. But she was really feeling very poorly.

She said, "It's so drizzly outside. Can't you wait until tomorrow?"

A few minutes later, Roy went out into the weather to get cigarettes. He was back home soon.

Kate thought, "Thank goodness. He beat the serious rain home. I should have forced myself to go."

The phone rang and Roy answered it. Then he headed toward the door.

Kate said, "Roy, where are you going?"

Roy answered, "That was Harriet. She asked me to get her newspaper for her."

Kate said, "You don't need to go out in this. It's raining cats and dogs,"

"I'm wet anyway. I'll just take her the paper," Roy replied, and he shuffled out the door.

That night Roy made the coffee before he went to bed. For years he had made it but recently he had been too weak. When Kate saw that he had made coffee the next morning, she thought, "He knew how sick I was feeling so had forced himself to make coffee before he went to bed." She turned it on and went in to wash up. She had to sit on the stool several times before she was finished with her morning ablutions. Then she went and fell back into bed. She went to sleep and woke up about 9:00 a.m. She couldn't remember ever sleeping this late in the morning. Roy was still in bed, but he, too, was moving around.

He said, "I really feel weak. I need to get up and go to the bathroom. Hope I can make it."

When he got into the hall he hung on the chair that Kate had dragged in to give her some support as she went to the bathroom. "This chair is a good idea. I'm not going to sit on it, just lean a little. I may not be able to get up," Roy said, and he went into the bathroom.

Pretty soon he came back into the bedroom. "Are you getting up?" he asked Kate.

"I haven't decided. What are you going to do?"

Roy was struggling with his clothes. "I think I'll go sit in my chair."

"Then I will get up, too," Kate said.

She had to smile a little as they fought with their clothes. "I turned the coffee on. It should be ready."

Roy said, "Should I bring you a cup?"

"No, I'll be out in a minute or two." She knew how hard it would be for him.

They spent the next two days lying around. One evening Roy fell in the living room. He and Kate worked at it but they couldn't get him up. Kate took a pillow and put it under his head. "Do you think I should call 911?"

"No, don't do that." Roy said. "I'm just going to sleep here tonight. I'll probably be okay in the morning."

Kate staggered in to bed. Roy would probably be dead in the morning but he had said not to call anyone.

When Kate woke up the next morning, she went into the bathroom and washed and then got dressed. She was afraid to look in the living room. She went down the hall and peeked around the corner. Roy was in his chair. "The coffee's made," he said.

The next few days they just existed. Sometimes they ate a few bites. When Billie called, Kate would say they were doing better. Then Lynn called. When he heard that his dad had fallen and they were both sick he went over after work. He took one look at Roy and called 911. The ambulance came and took him to the hospital. Lynn would go over after work and spend time with him. Kate was just unable to go. She couldn't believe it. She had been sick over eleven days. Finally she called Lynn. "When you go over to the hospital, I want to go with you." So that night he came by to get her.

She walked into Roy's room. He didn't recognize her. He was obviously 'out of it.' She reached out to take his hand but he snatched it away and turned his back to her. She had Lynn take her home.

That night when Lynn got home from the hospital, he called Billie and said if she wanted to see Dad while he was still alive, she should come as soon as possible. Liz called the hospital from South Dakota and asked if she should come and they told her 'not yet.'

It was Tuesday night when Lynn called Billie. Herb hadn't been feeling well, so he said, "We can't go. I'm not able to go."

Billie said, "I'll take the bus and rent a car. I'm going." She called the bus station and found out a bus left close to midnight. She went in and took a bath and started to pack a suitcase. Herb came in and watched her a minute. "If you insist on going, I'll drive the motor home.

Billie said, "Herb, you don't have to go, but I do. I can take the bus."

Herb said, "I'm going."'

Herb had been feeling so badly that Billie was afraid for him to go without seeing his doctors. He had two appointments for Thursday, but she wasn't willing to wait that long. She called off work. On Wednesday morning when the office opened, she called his doctors. Dr. Sims did not come in on Wednesday, but his nurse called the drugstore so Herb could get his prescriptions refilled. Dr. Hoover did agree to see him. When he heard of Herb's sudden bouts of lack of breath and weakness and had examined him thoroughly, he sent him in for tests. He told them that when they got to California to call to find out the results of the tests. He added, "Herb, if you have difficulty breathing you go directly to a hospital over there. This can be very serious. I'll know better after I get the results of the tests."

Billie really didn't think that Herb would be able to drive the motor home. The weather had been very windy. The Bounder was very difficult to drive in the wind. It had also snowed. She still said she would be willing to take the bus.

Herb said, "No, I'm driving the Bounder."

They left about 6:30 Wednesday evening and spent the night at Sunset Point. Billie did drive part of the way when they were out on the freeway, but Herb drove most of the way. The wind took a holiday and the air was still, making the handling of the motor home much easier than usual.

Wednesday night when Lynn went to see his dad, Roy was not lucid most of the time. Then he turned to Lynn and said, "Tell Kate I love her very much."

Roy passed away at 3:15 a.m. on Thursday morning. The hospital called Lynn instead of Kate. He came by and told her the next morning. They notified the mortuary and were told that they would take care of everything. Roy and Kate had paid for their funerals ahead of time. Lynn stayed with her for a few hours. He phoned many people. Elizabeth said she would make arrangements to come as quickly as she could. He called his children that lived in Washington so they could make arrangements to come to the funeral. He called Pat, who said he would be there in a few hours.

Kate said, "Lynn, you don't have to stay with me. I'm going to take a shower and get dressed. I'll be all right. I want to be alone for a few hours."

So Lynn left. He needed to go to work so he could take off the next few days.

Kate showered and got dressed when the phone rang. It was the Mortuary. They wanted Kate to come down and pick out a casket. Kate said, "I need to get a ride and then I'll be down."

She hung up the phone and was trying to decide who to call when a car pulled up in front. Wonder of wonders, it was her lovely grandson, Pat. He would take her. So off they went. They looked at different caskets. Kate was legally blind and Pat was colorblind, but they did make a choice. When they got back to the house, the Bounder was parked in the driveway.

Herb and Billie had arrived at Kate's house in the early afternoon. The house had been unlocked but empty. Billie called Lynn's work and was told that he was home because of a death in the family. She then called Lynn's house and he told her that Dad had passed away at 3:15 a.m. Some of Lynn's children were coming from Washington. They were driving a van and sharing the driving. Coming were Keegan and her husband, Jerry, along with their son, Grayson; Lance; Laren; Calyn, and his wife, Lisa; and Clint. They left Friday afternoon. They all hoped to be back for work and school by Tuesday morning.

Elizabeth was still in South Dakota. She wanted to come but they were in a great blizzard. No planes were flying out of the eastern part of the state. The roads were closed. Even if planes were flying, there was no way to get to the airport because it was snowing and blowing too hard. Frank had had a knee replaced in December. His blood had needed thinning but the doctor had gotten carried away, so now his blood was too thin. All around the new knee he was bleeding internally. He was told to stay off his leg as much as possible. Hopefully, the blood would be absorbed into his skin. Their children had come to their house over Christmas and had spent two days snowbound. Now, Liz and Frank were snowbound again. The only child able to get to their house was Bob. He had great equipment for moving around in the snow. Good thing! They had animals that needed feeding. The roads were not passable. The airplanes were not flying. The phones were working, and Liz and Kate spent time on the phone discussing the situation.

Darrell, a not very good yardman, who had been on drugs at one time, came to mow Kate's lawn. He did a very good job for a change. As he was leaving Herb was out messing with a water leak on the motor home. He found it, but before he could fix it he started gasping for air. Darrell wanted to talk. Herb wanted to sit down. He sat on the porch long enough to catch his breath and then went into the house. Billie called Dr. Hoover and asked for the results of the tests. She explained the lack of breath. He said he would get the results and call back.

Billie and her Mom went to the cemetery to sign the papers to have the grave opened and then to look for a dress for Kate to wear. Lynn had told Billie to have Mom out of the house by one o'clock. He was coming to wash walls and ceilings. Her house was cleaner than Billie's but Lynn wanted things as nice as possible.

Billie felt a little bad about leaving Herb alone but she knew Lynn would be over in a few minutes. She moved her dad's chair next to the phone, brought Herb a glass of water and a peanut butter sandwich and told him not to move while he was alone. She gave him a notepad to write down what Dr. Hoover told him when he called back and to write down any other calls that came when he was alone.

Herb was alone when Dr. Hoover called back. He told Herb he needed to go to the hospital but he couldn't drive himself since he might pass out while driving. He spelled out what the tests showed and told him to give the note to the doctor at the hospital since it would save a lot of time. He gave the medical term. It was DIC disseminated intraocular coagulation, an autoimmune response to severe trauma. Herb decided to sit and wait for Billie to get back.

When Lynn walked into the house, Herb said, "I wonder when Billie is getting back. Dr. Hoover told me to get to the hospital."

Lynn said, "I'll take you to the hospital. Let's go." He wrote a note and they headed to the Redlands Community Hospital.

Kate and Billie got back to the house at four o'clock in the afternoon. They had looked unsuccessfully for a new black dress for Kate to wear at Roy's funeral, had bought some prescriptions, and had been to the cemetery. They read the note when they got home. Because of Dr. Hoover's phone call Lynn had taken Herb to the hospital. Harriet had brought over donuts.

Billie called the hospital and asked for Herb Banning. They said he was in the emergency wing and had no phone. The doctor had not seen him yet. A few minutes later Lynn called back.

He said, "Don't come over. Herb seems fine. They will probably give him a prescription and send him home. They said the doctor would see him soon so we might meet each other on the way."

So Kate and Billie waited. Lynn got home a little after dark. They had admitted Herb. Billie was going to take her mom's car and go to the hospital but Kate remembered that Billie had night blindness so she made Lynn drive her over. They stayed a few minutes only. Herb just wanted to sleep. They should have made sure that Herb was fed before they left. One of the results of his illness was an inability to eat normally. For lunch he had part of a peanut butter sandwich and an apple. This had taken him over an hour. So he really needed nourishment but nothing was given to him that night.

Lynn and Billie went back to Kate's. At last, Lynn got started on what he came to do. He cleaned out all the kitchen cupboards. He took everything down and washed the insides of all the cupboards. Then he replaced most of the things. A few things he threw away. He then washed the cupboard doors, inside and out. He washed the walls and the ceiling of the kitchen. Billie went to bed close to midnight. Lynn and Kate were still cleaning.

Chapter 57

Saturday morning dawned bright and clear. Lynn's children were on the way from the Seattle area. Elizabeth was snowbound. Erin and her son, Daniel, were coming Sunday night by plane from Seattle. Julie, Andy, Elizabeth, and Ambree were coming from Flagstaff. Kate was stuck with making a decision. Should she plan on the funeral on Monday or Tuesday morning? The preacher had said he would be available on short notice, but the mortuary and cemetery wanted 24-hour notice. Elizabeth had bought a ticket. If she could get to the Watertown airport she could fly to Sioux Falls and get into Ontario airport at 9:30 Sunday night. If she didn't get there on Sunday she could take the same flight on Monday. Kate called her oldest daughter and asked her how badly she would feel if she missed the funeral.

Elizabeth said, "It will be all right. I'll try to get there but there is no guarantee that I will even get there on Monday night. I will come as soon as possible. Go ahead and have the funeral on Monday. I'll come as soon as I am able and will stay at least a week."

Billie spent Saturday at the hospital. They had not fed Herb the night before. He had not been fed that morning because more tests were being taken. One test had shown that he had blood clots on his lungs. At one time, his oxygen level was at 35 percent. He was put on heparin, a blood thinner, and oxygen. Finally he was fed at noon.

Lynn washed the living room walls and ceiling.

Sunday morning Billie went to the hospital.

Lynn, Gayanne, Lynn's children and Kate went to view Roy's body. His face was full. He had on his brown suit with his red tie. He looked so peaceful and pain free. He would be sorely missed but finally he was without pain for the first time in over thirty-five years. That was some solace that he was now with his blessed Savior in heaven. But oh, how empty and lonesome the house would be for Kate without him!

Pat and Sherrie came to their Grandma Kate's house in the afternoon. Julie and her family came soon after. Billie got home from the hospital about four o'clock. Everyone had been invited to Lynn and Gayanne's house for tacos. Pat, Sherrie and Christopher left. Then Julie's family and Billie left. They all stopped at the mortuary to view their grandpa and dad one last time. Then on they went to Lynn's house. Kate refused to go. She wanted to rest up for the following day. Julie and her family and Billie all stopped at the hospital to see Herb on the way to Lynn and Gayanne's house.

Elizabeth's Sunday was a little different. The airport called. Planes were flying. Bob came to the house and got the big tractor ready to plow. He plowed as far as he could. While he was still about thirty feet from another road that had been plowed, the tractor refused to go any further. Liz got out of the tractor and crawled-walked across the snow bank. She carried or pushed her luggage ahead of her. A kind neighbor met her on the other side of the snow bank and took her toward Watertown. He also had to plow part of the way. Eventually they got to a main road where the county had plowed and then they went on to Watertown. She hated to leave Frank with his leg propped up but Bob assured her that he would look in on him at least twice a day. He would also do the chores that were necessary. Frank told her to go and, of course, there was no way he could go with her.

Elizabeth took the flight to Sioux Falls and on to Ontario, California. Lynn picked her up and put her up for the night. Some of his children and Pat's family were all staying at a Redland motel. Erin also caught a flight from Washington on Sunday. She got in at 10:30 at night and rented a motel close to the airport. Billie and Julie's bunch went back to Kate's house about 9:00. People were finding places to sleep.

Monday morning a soft rain was falling. Billie thought it was angels crying for the loneliness that Kate would feel. Lynn's daughter, Kelly, came to the house. She had come to California for a baby shower of a close friend and stayed over for the funeral. Erin and Daniel came to the house. Pat, Sherrie, Christopher, and Sherrie's parents came to the house. Lynn, Gayanne, and Elizabeth came. Then they all went to the funeral.

Billie held Julie's daughter Elizabeth, called Bizy, who was three years old. Bizy was so happy sitting popping a lid on and off a film can; pop, pop, pop. Billie was afraid that Kate would find the noise distracting so she took the can away. Bizy fussed so Billie handed her back to her mom on the second row. Bizy continued fussing, so Julie had Andy take the two little girls out. How Bizy cried. Billie could hear her through the walls.

She felt so bad. The popping was a soft little sound and had kept her so happy. How Roy had loved his grandchildren and great grandchildren. If he knew about the popping he would rather have enjoyed having the little ones at his funeral.

Roy and Kate's grandchildren did so well at the funeral. Pat played the organ. Calyn and his wife, Lisa, sang "Sweet Hour of Prayer" and "Amazing Grace." Lynn's Keegan was the hostess. Preacher George Bedlion gave the talk. Lynn gave the eulogy.

LEROY C. MILLER
June 24, 1910 - Jan. 9, 1997
EIGHTY SIX YEARS ON EARTH

We\ are here to acknowledge the passing of LEROY C. MILLER. A man that traveled this earth for 86 and one half years. A man that owes no apologies to anyone and left nothing unfinished. His main function was to love and raise his family and love and care for his wife. Mom said two nights ago she never saw a man who loved his children more than dad. This wonderful love has been passed down from generation to generation. The torch has now been passed from dad to his children with the obligation to pass it on.

Leroy was a son, husband and father. He was also a school teacher. He taught school in Colorado, Arizona and California for 45 years to support his family.

I would not only like to acknowledge my dad this morning. I would also like to pay respects to his generation. A generation that built the United States into the country that is the envy of the world.

Dad's generation invented and mass produced the automobile and the airplane, without which my sisters and children would not have been able to be here with my Mother and I to celebrate the life of my dad. In his lifetime, he saw us break the sound barrier and conquer space. His generation fought two world wars, paved the highways, built schools, hospitals, and towns that grew into cities. In his life, he saw the atom split and the mother of all inventions, the microchip. I would like to thank my dad's generation for giving us this great country to live in. Thank you.

LEROY THE SCHOOL TEACHER

For my dad's part in the scheme, he chose to teach. His seven brothers and sisters as well as his cousins and in-laws became farmers, accountants, preachers, laborers and all the other professions that make an organized society. But my Dad was a teacher. He started in a one-room school house north of Lymon, Colorado in 1928. He was 18 years old. His students were children of farmers, with few social graces and little money. Those were the years leading to the Great Depression. Eighteen year old Leroy Miller taught them, counseled them and even cut the boys hair and sometimes curled that of the girls.

Leroy Miller finished his teaching career in Pico Rivera, where he taught for 15 years, retiring in 1975 when he was 65. He taught nearly 4000 students how to play basketball and a lot about math. Mainly he taught them they were valuable to him and to themselves, a quality that set him high in the ranks as a person.

LEROY THE SON

My dad was the second of eight children and the oldest son of Lewis and Suzy Miller. My grandfather was a Mennonite preacher, a farmer, and a school teacher; a beloved man and someone his son, Leroy, looked up to with respect all of his life.

When the Millers got a new horse drawn carriage in the early 1920s, Leroy, about 12 years old and his younger brother, Frank, took their father's straight razor and cut strips in the canvas cover, giving the carriage a lot of class and the look of a zebra. "The worst punishment I got" he said. "Dad spanked us with green onion stems." My Dad and Frank still thought the carriage was better off for the efforts of their customizing.

LEROY THE FATHER

Leroy fathered five children; my sisters are Elizabeth who had 5 children and 15 grandchildren, Helen Ann whom we lost a few years ago, had 2 children and 6 grandchildren, Billie who has 2 children and 9 grandchildren and Kathleen who died as a young teenager. I have an extended family of 13 children and 14 grandchildren. Leroy and Katherine Miller had 5 children and 45 grandchildren and the number is growing. Leroy knew every grandchild's name, how old they are and they all knew him as being a very special person. He, like the prophet Abraham, has a 'quiver that is full.'

In 1942 Leroy Miller moved his family from Colorado to Casa Grande, Arizona then to Flagstaff for two years. He was the most non-violent man I have ever known yet taught judo in the Navy program at the college in Flagstaff for the war effort. Yuma was the next Miller home for two years after which they settled in Mesa for 15 wonderful years. They arrived there in a huge black Packard that gave up the ghost the next day. We kids used to love that car because it had jump seats that pulled down in back, so for a family of seven there was plenty of room.

Besides teaching and coaching, my Dad milked cows while we were in Mesa. He milked the cows to put his children through college. As Liz pointed out last night, 'a good education for his children was not an option.' As you can see, my Dad was a man that accepted the responsibility of being a father without hesitation, and there was never a question as to who was going to support his family.

LEROY THE HUSBAND

Katherine Troyer was married to Leroy on August 14, 1931. His last coherent words to me, his son, on January 8, 1997 was, "tell Kate I love her very much." a reinforcement of a commitment he had made over 65 years ago, and from which he never wavered.

GOODBYE OUR FRIEND

We will miss you Dad. Gayanne, my sisters and our children share in these sentiments and we thank you for your examples. We thank you for your love. We thank you for your friendship and the way you stayed active in the lives of your children and grandchildren. We thank you for being with us these last 86 years and we are looking forward to seeing you when our life on earth is over. Goodbye and thank you.

 The grandsons were the pallbearers. Clint rode in the hearse with his Grandpa. Pat made Kate's neighbor, Harriet, feel so good by offering his arm and walking her up to see Roy and then walking her out to her car.

 Perry's daughter, Breta and her husband were at the funeral but were heading back home to Venice, California. Kate's niece, Evon, was there. The graveside service was very short because the rain was pouring down. Once again, Lynn and Gayanne opened their home. Everyone ate and visited. Gayanne's daughter, Lynda had prepared lots of delicious food. People started back to their homes after the gathering. Erin and her son headed back to the airport at five o'clock. By that time Lynn's children were headed back to Seattle. They all planned to go back to school and work on Tuesday. They weren't sure how they were going home because the rains had caused highway 5 to be closed in a few places.

Julie and her family headed home so Andy would not miss too much work. Also, it might take them a while to get home because of the snowy Flagstaff weather. Elizabeth and Billie spent a week with their Mother. Billie missed very little school because the Flagstaff schools were closed for five days because of the snow.

Elizabeth went through papers and discarded old utility bills and other worthless documents. She cleaned drawers and tried to make her mom's life less complicated. She and Billie also made numerous phone calls about social security, insurance, and Roy's retirement. Billie copied phone numbers much bigger and darker so that Kate could see them when she was alone.

Nathaniel Gee, his great grandson, wrote a poem soon after his death;

Elegy to L. C. Miller

In the hospital bed, he gasped for air
She leaned and took his misshapen hand and sighed,
"You can go, Roy. I know you truly care,
I'm okay," His eyes fluttered and he died.
She turned to her friends and family
"For me he lived ten years longer than he ought
Who would take care of me, he couldn't foresee."
Tears in her eyes as she expressed her thought.

Leroy Miller was a wonderful man
He was a great grandfather when he died
He was the beloved leader of his clan
They all miss him, especially his bride.

My great grandma Miller lives alone now
At 86 for the very first time
It's been a year and she's getting along somehow
I'm glad they had such love in their lifetime.

Roy had been in pain for many years because of the terrible car wreck back in the fifties. In the later years, he had fulfilled three big needs for Kate. The first was companionship and caring. The other two were reading the mail and writing the checks and finally, when Dial-a-Ride was not convenient, he would drive her places. Because of the macular degeneration she could not read, write, or drive.

Kate enjoyed her books on tape from the Braille Institute. Pat and Sherrie had also bought meals on wheels three days a week for their grandparents.

On the 14th, Herb was released from the Redlands Community Ho spital. He spent the rest of the week sitting around and watching lots of television.

Billie's daughter, Katherine, did not come to the funeral from Wisconsin. She didn't feel she could make the trip twice and thought her visit to her grandmother would be more beneficial in March. So two months later, she flew into the airport, rented a car and drove to Yucaipa. This was an excellent decision because Kate was feeling quite lonesome and in the doldrums in March. She and Kathy had a lovely visit and then Kate was alone again.

Chapter 58

Kate was lonely. Her Braille tape player kept tearing up the tapes so Kate had had it sent back to the Institute for a replacement. Not only had no replacement been sent but the tapes quit coming. Her television still worked but she much preferred the talking books. Kate called the institute. Billie called the institute. Pat called the institute. But she did not get a tape player or tapes.

Lynn and Gayanne began coming every Sunday and meeting her at church. She would take the church van and go to Sunday school first. Then they would meet and go to the church service. Afterwards, they would go out to eat. Then they would go to Kate's house and visit, and Gayanne would read the mail and write any checks for bills that had come in. How Kate looked forward to Sundays.

During the week, she mostly just wanted to sleep. Before the tape player broke, she would lie in bed and listen to tapes. Now she would just lie on the bed.

Darrell still came weekly to cut the grass. But Kate noticed a change and it was not for the better. He worked much more carelessly than when Roy was alive. He was rude to her and tried to come into the house. She still gave him a big glass of water and had him help himself to any fruit that was ripe. He, in return, cut her hose, pulled down her automatic garage door by brute strength thus getting it off the track, and did a haphazard job on the lawn.

Finally, Kate decided to replace him. She hated to, in a way, because she knew he was an 'over comer' that had been on drugs at one time. But the last time he came he brought a surly young man with him. Kate was quite uncomfortable while they were in her yard. She told Darrell that she did not want him to come anymore. How Darrell grumbled and mumbled, "I need this job. I can't pay my bills," and said quite a bit more along the same lines. Kate went into the house and closed and locked the two outside doors.

Then she began asking around. She got the name of a fireman that mowed lawns on his off day. She called him and the next week he came with his wife. She told him what she wanted done and paid him for the coming month and went into the house. She was a little upset by the request to pay a month in advance, but she did.

When he showed up to mow and rake her yard, it seemed like the fireman and his wife were there for a very short time. When they left, she went out into her yard. She was pleased. They had done a much better job than Darrell had ever done.

Jeannie came once a month and did the extra cleaning. Kate wanted her to clean the things that needed it that Kate missed because of her poor eyesight. She also vacuumed and would clean the bathroom. The rest of the month, Kate forced herself to clean a little every day. She would also go into the yard and do a little yard work. She wasn't interested in eating but she would sit down and eat something every day.

Billie would call every evening, but Kate just hadn't realized she depended on Roy so much. She knew he had held on to his life much by will power, because he couldn't see how she could cope alone. He'd known better than she had. She'd learned the phone numbers of Dial-a-Ride and the church van. She'd been taking Dial-a-Ride to buy groceries for the longest time. But after being married over sixty-five years, love and companionship taken for granted and now no longer available, left a gut-wrenching emptiness.

After her granddaughter Kathy's visit in March the days were unbearable. The loneliness had faded when Kathy was there. They had been busy running around and eating out and she was such a pleasant, intelligent woman it had been a very nice time. Then she was gone. The days were empty and long.

Chapter 59

When Ann had died, Bill had brought over their little two-foot tall live Christmas tree. Even though it was the end of February, Ann had not yet decided where she would plant it. Kate and Roy talked about it and planted it about six feet in front of their big picture window of the living room. At first, it didn't do very well and was quite brown at the bottom. Then one morning, Kate looked out the window and saw one of many loose morning dogs of the neighborhood peeing on the tree. She grabbed her broom and ran out and chased it away. That afternoon she and Roy had sprayed a repellent around the base of the tree, so the dogs would not bother it. That did the trick and the tree began to grow and grow and grow. They both headed for the tree every morning to see if they could tell if it had grown. It was amazing. It seemed as though it grew noticeably every day.

The roots spread out and they worried about the foundation of the house. They decided that they were deep enough so as not to bother it. At least that is what they hoped. In what seemed like a relatively short time the two foot tree had grown much higher than the house with a trunk as thick as a barrel. It was outside her big front room window. After Roy died, Kate enjoyed having the tree there because she realized that it afforded additional privacy without the drapes being closed.

One day in April, Kate looked out her front door. There was Rooster. He strutted across her lawn looking cocky. Kate called her neighbor, Harriet. "Have you seen or heard about this rooster that is strutting in my front yard?"

Harriet said, "Kate, I have no idea what you are talking about."

Kate called her neighbor that lived on her north side and repeated the question.

Maude said, "He's been strutting up and down the street for a week."

Kate hung up the phone. She got some bread and a big bowl. She put both outside her window by the big tree. She took the hose and filled the bowl. He was very thirsty. He drank and drank and then nibbled at the bread. Then he flew up into the big tree. For the first time since she had been alone, she smiled. The next morning at four o'clock she heard him crow. How wonderful! When she had worked, her alarm clock had crowed to wake her. Now, she had the real thing.

Every morning at 4:00 when he would crow five times to greet the morning, she would listen, smile and go back to sleep. The first few times she had gotten up and gotten him something to eat. By the time she would get outside, he would be back to roosting in Ann's tree. So now she would count his crows and go back to sleep. He would crow again close to 6:00. This time he would crow until she took him something to eat.

Rooster never let Kate touch him, but he would 'talk' to her when she fed him. He would announce visitors and follow her when she walked around in the front yard. The first Sunday after he came, Gayanne had taken her to get him some hamster food. Rooster approved.

One day Kate had gone to Harriet's to help her put on clean sheets. They'd finished and were sitting down to a cup of tea, when Harriet noticed a frantic rooster running back and forth between her gate and her door. Kate jumped up and went out to see what was wrong. She tried to calm him down but to no avail. She decided to try to get him back to his/her tree. She opened Harriet's gate. Rooster scooted through it and stopped. He puffed up his chest and feathers. He flapped his wings and crowed and crowed. Then he strutted back home.

Kate loved her backyard and got in the habit of going out the front door and around the house and through the gate into the backyard. Rooster would follow her until she got to the gate. Then he would stop. She would go on into the backyard and leave the gate open but nothing could entice him into the gated and fenced yard.

Occasionally, Rooster would strut up and down the avenue, but at night he'd be back in the tree. Kate realized that when the television was on he'd sit down low. He did not move up high in the tree until she'd turn it off after the game shows, Jeopardy and Wheel of Fortune. These were the two programs that she and Roy had watched together. She turned the television toward the window and moved her chair out of his line of vision. When Billie called, Kate said, "I'm not alone anymore."

The neighbors began complaining. It seemed that others did not share her love of the crow of a rooster at four o'clock in the morning. She paid little attention. She said, "I don't know why they don't just sleep on their good ear."

She'd usually be up, so as soon as he started crowing for his breakfast, she would be out there with food. As soon as she fed him, he would stop crowing and eat. One of the worst complainers had a dog that barked late into the night and would be turned loose to relieve himself on her open front yard early in the morning. She ignored the complaints.

One day she saw a city pick-up with a cage in the bed of the truck. She didn't know where Rooster was right at the moment and only hoped he would stay out of sight. If he was in the tree, he was high and quiet. Maybe he recognized the function of the truck and would stay hidden. The pick-up was driven up and down the street a few times and then left. How Kate hoped that was the end of it.

Then it happened. Billie called and was greeted with, "My rooster's gone."

Billie was sad. She knew how important he'd been to her Mom. "The city picked him up?"

Kate said, "No, a dog. I heard this squealing. By the time I got to the door, the dog was just disappearing around the hedge with something in his mouth. There were turkey feathers everywhere." Kate was desolate.

Four days dragged by. Finally, Kate was once again getting Braille tapes. The old player had been replaced and tapes were no longer being destroyed. But they were boring. She was more lonesome than ever.

Then Maude, her ninety-five year old neighbor, came walking up the hill and around the hedge. Following behind her was Rooster. A wing was dragging, feathers were missing, he looked bedraggled, but it was Rooster.

Kate started toward him. He turned away. So she went and sat on her steps. Maude said, "He was in my front yard. So I said, 'Let's go see Katherine' and he followed me. He keeps about three feet between us at all times."

While they were talking, Rooster went to the tree. He jumped onto a lower branch and laboriously jumped from limb to limb to the top of the tree.

That night when Billie called, she couldn't believe the happiness in Kate's voice, "My rooster's back. He didn't die. Someone must have freed him from the dog. He's back in my tree."

Rooster was back but he was angry and frightened. Kate would put out food and water. He would wait until she went back into the house before he would come down. After he finished eating, back to the top of the tree he'd go. There was no more crowing.

Time passed. Then one morning, he crowed. It was pretty weak, but it was music to Kate's ears. Eventually, he would eat if she'd stay sitting on the step. One day he walked over and gave her a whack with his wing. Kate knew he was saying, "Why didn't you protect me from that dog."

Rooster had never let Kate touch him. He would get quite close to her, but if she put out a hand he would retreat. He would come close whenever she was outside. He would announce visitors, but ignored the mailman that would drop Kate's mail through the slot in the door.

Geneva, who lived to the south of Kate in the big house in front of Harriet's little apartment made cornbread quite often. When she made a batch, she got in the habit of giving Rooster a piece about the size of a slice of bread. When she brought the cornbread over, she could pet the big bird. But Kate was never allowed to touch him.

It was over a month since he had moved back into the big tree. Then one night,

Kate glanced out her window and he was back watching television with her. Kate's smile stretched from ear to ear.

Kate always enjoyed getting mail. She didn't know why. It was mostly bills and advertisements. But often, she would get a letter from her grandchild, Kathy or Kathy's daughter, Keegan. One day a letter came from the city. How she wondered what it was about. She was anxious for Gayanne to read it to her on Sunday. When Gayanne read it aloud the following Sunday, the line that stuck in Kate's head was, "You have until June 16 to get rid of your rooster."

"Get rid of it. What do they want me to do? Shoot it? He's never allowed me to touch him." Kate asked Lynn and Gayanne in person and Billie on the phone.

The sixteenth of June came. A woman from the city knocked on Kate's door. "Your neighbors are complaining. We're going to have to do something." This time Rooster strutted out to meet and announce her but he didn't let her get close enough to touch him.

Kate straightened up to her full five feet. "I don't know why. Nothing is done about the crows that eat my garden. Nothing is done about the dogs that yap all night and go in my yard for me to pick it up. Nothing is done about the jays that screech and call. He's never let me touch him. He's just as free as the other birds that are around my yard."

The city worker struggled to keep a straight face. "What should I do when the neighbors call and complain?"

"Just listen and say you'll look into it and then forget it."

A week later when Billie and Herb came to visit, Rooster crowed to let Kate know she had company but Kate was at church so they stayed in the motor home and waited. They had brought over a car dolly so they could take Kate's 1978 Chrysler LeBaron back with them. They disconnected the dolly and pushed and pulled it on the grass out of the street. When Kate, Lynn, and Gayanne came from church they moved the car out of the garage and parked it on the lawn, also. Then Herb backed the motor home into the driveway. They would need the car to drive around and the motor home filled the driveway.

The next morning Rooster crowed and crowed and crowed. The car and dolly were in his strutting place. There was still a lot of lawn left but, obviously, that mattered little to him. How he objected. He objected loudly and strenuously for four days. Even the neighbors that loved Kate and knew how important Rooster was to her were beginning to wish Herb and Billie would go home. By the fourth day he was a little quieter and would even come down out of the tree if they were in the front yard. They stayed a week. After they left, how Rooster strutted. He was so proud that he had gotten them to leave. There was no doubt in Kate's mind that he was bragging about his powers and accomplishments. He reverted immediately back to his five crows at four a.m. and crowing until Kate fed him at six o'clock.

When Geneva had a lot of company and some of them parked on her lawn, Rooster objected loudly. Apparently, he had to tell people that they were to park on the driveways only and never on the grass. When the company left how he would strut and crow to let everyone know he was responsible for their leaving. The rest of the time he was on his best behavior. July came and went and Kate heard no more from the city.

The days went by. Rooster was eating well. He had trained Kate to only feed him foods he liked. When Kate would now give him hamster food or some bird seeds, he would scatter them to show his displeasure. Geneva would occasionally give him a piece of cornbread which seemed to be a favorite food, but the rest of the time he was content with the seeds that he had trained Kate to buy.

August and September went by. Kate was once again the content person she had been most of her life. She saw Lynn and Gayanne every Sunday. Tim was an outstanding yard person. Her yard looked very nice, only Maude's looked better because it was such a lovely green. Rooster was eager to see her in the morning and when she came home from church or shopping. He was getting very protective of her property and would loudly announce visitors and run and hiss at people that would walk on the edge of her property. Her grass went right to the street and if a car was coming people would step on her grass. How Rooster objected. If they would walk up to the door, he would crow but not run at them.

Kate was becoming very concerned about the coming winter. She had tried several times to get Rooster to spend the nights in her garage but he wanted no part of being closed in anywhere. He would not even go into the backyard when the gate was left open. So he wasn't about to go into the garage even if the door was left open. Doors and gates could be closed.

Billie and Herb came again in October. On the sixteenth, Kate would be eighty-eight years old. When they drove into the yard Rooster crowed again and again. He had never looked better. His tail was flowing behind him in a dazzling array. He was a picture of good health. He crowed and crowed so Kate knew she had company.

Billie and Herb took their two toy poodles to the back yard and turned them loose. How Shadow loved to run after the long trip in the motor home. Cookie, on the other hand, would relieve herself and want in the house.

Since it was Sunday and they were early enough, Billie went to church with Kate. Herb stayed in the motor home to shave and clean up. After church, he would go to lunch with them and Lynn and Gayanne.

While Herb was shaving, Rooster realized that there were creatures in Kate's back yard. For the first time ever, he went into the back yard. He flew over the four foot chain link gate and flew at the intruders. He probably would have been more successful if there had been only one dog, but there were two. Shadow and Cookie had spent quite a bit of time in Kate's backyard and they knew this creature had no right to be there. Quite a fight ensued. Somehow, Shadow and Rooster ended up in the front yard. Cookie was barking, Rooster was screeching, and Shadow had a mouthful of something that was flapping and pecking and making outlandish noises. A crowd was forming. One resourceful neighbor brought a towel and rescued the bird and wrapped him up to protect him from the black dog. Shadow was jumping and barking and Herb finally heard the chaos and came and put the two dogs back into the motor home. Cookie was all right but Shadow plopped down on the couch exhausted. The young woman with the bird told Herb where she lived and added, "Tell Katherine I'll keep the rooster until she comes and gets him."

When the rest of them came from church to pick Herb up to go out and eat, Katherine lost all interest in food. She went over to pick up Rooster. The woman that had rescued him was new in the neighborhood and Kate had never spoken to her or her husband except to say 'hi.' She had no idea how she even knew her name. She gave the rooster to Kate, and Kate carried him back to her own yard. She put him into the back yard which had a goodly supply of turkey feathers everywhere. She left the gate open. She poured hydrogen peroxide on all the open wounds and put him in a leafy part of the back yard. The dogs were secure in the motor home.

Kate decided that they would go out to eat and give him a chance to rest. After eating they stopped to buy more hydrogen peroxide and went back to the bird. He was restless in the back yard so Kate carried him to the big tree and put him on the bottom branch. He fell or jumped down. He was still walking and he wasn't about to stay there with the motor home and the dogs and extra people especially since they had seen his embarrassing situation. He headed slowly up the hill toward Geneva's house.

Kate said, "Let him go. I never have kept him against his will."

What a sleepless night Kate spent. He would be helpless against the dogs roaming the street. The next morning Billie walked up and down the street and finally spotted him. He was squeezed in behind the wheelbarrow on Geneva's porch.

Every night he would sleep somewhere else. Every day, Kate would walk quietly around the house and yard looking for him. He would walk around but he did not come back to Kate's yard or the tree. Finally, Wednesday night he came home and slept inside the garage. Kate had left the door open and had put food and water inside the garage hoping he would come back. She also put a small step stool out under the tree to enable him to get back up into the tree.

Thursday night he was across the street inside a yard and Herb saw the elderly woman who lived in the house shoving Rooster with a broom. Herb and Billie went over to herd him back home. Rooster left the yard that was surrounded by chain link fencing but he wasn't about to let these two strangers tell him where to go. He took off up the hill away from Kate's yard.

Friday he was again walking around in Geneva's and Kate's yards. He would run up hill if anyone came out of Kate's house. But he did spend time under the tree when the yard was empty. Then Herb looked out and saw him again in the fence across the street. The elderly woman and two small children were standing on the porch.

Billie said to Kate, "Mom, they really don't like Rooster and he objects to Herb and me telling him where to go. Don't you think you should go and get him?"

So Kate went across the street. The grandma went into the house. When Kate tried to herd Rooster, he was unable to walk. He would fall over whenever he tried to take a step. So once again, Kate picked up the sixteen pound bird and carried him back to her backyard. He had no fight left. He just sat. The next time she went out she opened the garage door that went into the back yard but could not see Rooster anywhere. The next morning he was sitting by the garage door. He could hardly move. Kate gave him water which he drank and offered him food which he refused. She poured more hydrogen peroxide on any open wounds. Kate surmised that the woman across the street had beaten him, but she was only protecting her grandchildren.

Saturday, Rooster moped around. Herb had to get back to work so they decided to go home. Kate was relieved that they were going. The motor home, the car, the dogs, the extra people all caused Rooster stress, especially in his condition.

After they left Kate sat in the back yard with Rooster. He just sat. Now Kate could touch him. She petted him. Kate went into the house at dark. She had left the big overhead garage door open and also the door into the back yard. She had also left the gate into the back yard open. If Rooster got to feeling better and wanted to go into the front yard, she wanted him to be able to do that. She checked on him before she went to bed and could not find him. Good, maybe he had found a warm place to spend the night.

The next morning Kate went out to check on him. He was lying dead by the garage door. Kate was bereft. She went into the house and got dressed. She went into her back yard and dug a hole. She wrapped him into a sheet and buried him in the yard. Then she went into the house and sat in her chair. She called Lynn and said, "I'm not going to church today."

Lynn and Gayanne went to church and then stopped by. They had brought lunch. For the first time Kate was glad when they had left. By the next Sunday she would be able to cope, but today she just wanted to feel sad and to think of the happiness Rooster had brought her during a very hard time.

Chapter 60

In the period after Rooster died, Kate was very lonely. Then one day, she told herself, "You have to snap out of this depression." Her children were talking about having her go to live with one of them, which she had long ago decided that she would never do. She knew if she wanted to stay in her house, she would have to show that this was the best solution for right now. So she began to go back to being her independent self. If any of her children talked about her coming to live with them, she would reply, "I'm going to live here for two more years."

Lynn and Gayanne had been coming every Sunday, then Lynn was coming alone. Gayanne had flown to Florida to work for her sister, Judy. Judy had a consulting firm and needed someone to help her. The economy in California was not very good. The money Gayanne made working for Judy was quite a bit better than the money they were making in California. When Southwest Airlines had special one way flights for $99 or less, Gayanne would fly back to California for a few days. But they didn't like this living apart and having two places of residence.

One night Lynn called Billie. "Now that you've retired, why don't you and Herb move to California. I don't see how we can leave Mom alone. Things are bad in California. I would like to move to Florida with Gayanne but I don't see how we can leave Mom here. She loves her house and really doesn't want to move."

Billie said, "Herb is still barbering. I love Flagstaff. I just don't want to move. Maybe mom will move here. I'll start looking for a place for her to stay."

So one Sunday, Lynn broke the news to Kate. He was moving to Florida. Gayanne was making good money. They were almost sixty years old and had nothing set aside for their old age. She and Judy worked well together. The business was growing and Lynn knew he could find some kind of job out there. He was tired of being in California with Gayanne in Florida. They would save the money Gayanne spent on flights. They would gladly take Kate with them. She could have her own room and bathroom in their house. They would get along well together.

How Kate hated to hear this, but at the same time she was a little relieved for their sake. She loved Gayanne and she knew it wasn't good for these two to live apart. She said, "Go. I'll do just fine. I'm going to live in this house for two more years."

Lynn said, "How can you do that? You can't see to read your mail or get around."

Kate answered, "I've got Dial-a-Ride and I saw this coming. Jeannie is going to come once a week to write my checks and read my mail to me. She can't clean anymore. She has had surgery and is quite weak, but I like her and she can read and write."

Gayanne's daughter, Lynda, was very unhappy about the permanent move to Florida. She was visibly upset and when Kate saw how sad it made Gayanne, she decided that she would not let them see how sad it would make her. She would tell them, "I'm fine. I have meals on wheels and Dial-a-Ride and I have Jeannie. I'm going to live here two more years."

They moved and Kate was desolate. She only saw them on Sundays but she had known that they were close by. Now they were clear across the country. But she would be fine because, if she lived by herself, she would have to be.

Chapter 61

The days were lonely. When it was time for the meals on wheels to be delivered, she would start watching for the van. A silent young man would knock and hand her the lunch in a sack. Then he would leave. She would always thank him but he said nothing.

The lunches were much more than she would eat at a meal. So there was plenty for supper, too. Often she would eat the dessert the following day. For breakfast she ate a piece of bread and butter and preserves or apple butter and would have a cup of coffee. Cooking for herself was not fun.

She was glad for her automatic washing machine but she still would hang her clothes on the line outside. One night, she remembered that she had not brought in the clothes from the line. She decided that even though it was dark, she would go and get them. So off she went. As she got out to the line, she tripped over the galvanized tub that was by the clothesline. She used it to bring in her clothes. She couldn't believe it. In she fell. Her seat was in the tub. Her feet and arms were out, but try as she might, she couldn't lift herself out. She put her hands on the top of the tub, but she couldn't pull herself out. She put her arms inside the tub and pushed on the bottom. But she had no luck. She was stuck.

She wasn't comfortable but it was bearable. She was thinking, "What if I have to stay here all night? It will get mighty cold. Maybe one of my neighbors will come and then I'll yell for help. At least the stars are out nice and bright. I always did like the night sky."

All the time she was thinking, she was trying to get out of the tub. Then she had another idea. She'd try to tip it over. She leaned over to her right. She felt it tip a little. So she slid as far to the right as she could. Then she leaned and stretched and leaned to the right. She felt the left side lift up so she threw herself to the right. Sure enough, it tipped over and dumped her on the grass. She decided her clothes could wait until tomorrow. She went back into the house. She looked at the clock. She had been in the tub for over two hours. The back of her knees were scratched but it felt good to be safe inside her house.

Chapter 62

For her 88th birthday, Billie drove to Yucaipa and they had a van come to the door and take them to the airport. They then flew out to Orlando and rented a car and drove to Melbourne, Florida to spend a week with Lynn and Gayanne. Kate made Billie promise not to leave her there. She did not want to live with one of her children. So off they went. When they got to the airport in San Bernadino and found where they were to go just as they got to one of the security gates, Kate fell. What activity that caused. She was not hurt but she did end up being given preferential treatment and she was loaned a wheelchair. From then on she and Billie were put at the head of the line.

They spent a week in Florida. The time sped by. Kate rather wished they could stay a few more weeks. Lynn had a nice home in a senior citizen park. They had a screened in porch where they could watch the people walk their dogs and walk for exercise. Everyone was very friendly. They had a kitchen, dining room, family room, two bedrooms, two bathrooms, and a living room that was seldom used.

On Saturday, Lynn took Billie kayaking while Gayanne took Kate to get a manicure and a pedicure. They all went out to eat. One night they went and ate at Gayanne's sister Judy's house. It was a lovely evening. Other nights, Gayanne would get everything ready before she left for work in the morning. It was a very nice time. Lynn once again invited his mother to live with them. Kate gave them her standard answer, "I'm going to live in my house for two more years." So back to the plane they went. When they got back to California, they again took a van to Kate's door.

Chapter 63

Aaron, a fifth grader, who lived across the street and up a few houses had gotten into the habit of stopping by almost every day to talk to Kate. How she looked forward to his visits. He talked about what his twin sisters, Samantha and Michaela, were doing in school and things that happened at home. His mother, Michelle, was going to college and working in a classroom. Aaron introduced Kate to Pokemon and Harry Potter. His visits were the highlight of her days.

Her neighbor, ninety-nine year old Maude, had died and her children had sold her house. The young man who had bought it, brought her a lemon crème cake that was a very nice treat. He had always lived in an apartment and was a little surprised at the amount of work a house and yard took. But he tackled it good naturedly and kept it the best looking house and yard on the street. Since Tim had started taking care of Kate's yard it was a close second. Geneva would bring her asparagus or corn bread once in a while. She had good neighbors.

About every six months, Billie and Herb came out in the motor home. Then Herb decided that he just didn't want to go. So Billie started going out by herself. Kate always worried when Billie was on the road between Flagstaff and Yucaipa. She drove a 1997 Nissan that they had bought new, so Billie felt pretty secure in it.

Then one night Billie got a call. It was Jeannie. She had taken Kate to the Redlands Hospital. The next morning, Billie took off for California.

Kate had hemorrhaged. She had lost a lot of blood and was quite ill. Billie spent the day with her. That evening from Kate's house, she called Herb, Julie, Kathy, Pat, Erin, Lynn, and Elizabeth. Much of the day Kate had not been lucid. The doctors did not seem very concerned, but Billie was.

Kate was tough and in a few days she was sent home. She was told to stay in bed and elevate her legs. This wasn't hard. By Sunday night the pain in her legs was unbearable. One leg was very swollen and the other was a little swollen. Billie, fearing blood clots, called 911.

The paramedics said take Advil and go to the doctor tomorrow. So the next day, off they went. Billie went in and got a wheelchair at the doctor's office since they had to park a ways away. The doctor said, "Keep your feet elevated and take Advil." Kate's insurance was an HMO.

Elizabeth came from South Dakota and so the three of them were there at Kate's house. Kate had been thinking. As she lay in bed she knew she would have to make some decisions. Herb had quit coming with Billie. She hated having Billie make that trip by herself. Her house had a new roof. She had a charitable organization that came weekly and took things away that she no longer used. She did so hate to leave this house. Kate thought about all the assisted living facilities in the vicinity. She had friends that had moved to one quite close by and they were content. But Kate knew that if she moved into one in Yucaipa, Billie would still be on the highway way too often.

Kate said, "I don't think that I can live alone anymore. I am going to need to sell my house."

Kate tried to follow the doctor's directions and stay off her feet as much as possible. She was in pain, but since the paramedics and the doctor were not concerned, she tried not to complain. On Wednesday afternoon, a nurse from the Redland's Hospital made a follow-up visit. She took one look at Kate's leg and asked her for her doctor's name. She then called the doctor and said that she feared a blood clot and he needed to make arrangements for her to get tested to make sure one way or the other.

He said, "Have her come in."

So Elizabeth and Billie bundled her in the car and went to the doctor. This time he called the clinic to get the tests but they said that it was too close to closing time. He suggested that they bring Kate in the next day and Billie said, "No, we were here yesterday. We have called the paramedics. It is very difficult and painful for Kate to move around. We need this to be taken care of now."

So the doctor sent them to the Redland's hospital where they waited for four hours. They then tested Kate for blood clots and she did indeed have them. Kate was lying on a bed in the emergency room and had gone to sleep. The doctor told Billie and Elizabeth to go home because they were going to admit her. They promised to call if there was any change, so Billie and Elizabeth went back to Kate's house.

Kate was in a hospital room when Elizabeth and Billie went to the hospital the next day. Soon after they got there, so did Pat from San Diego. A nurse in the hospital said to him, "You sure look a lot like Dustin Hoffman."

Pat said, "I've been told that before."

Kate was quite ill. Elizabeth, Pat, and Billie took turns talking to Kate. Kate was seldom conscious. When she was semiconscious she spent the afternoon singing hymns; "This World Is Not My Home" and "When the Roll Is Called Up Yonder" and other songs about going home to heaven. Her blood pressure dropped very low. She seemed a little better that evening so the three decided to go get something to eat. They went to a Korean Restaurant and ate strange but quite delicious food. Pat went back to San Diego. Billie and Elizabeth went back to Yucaipa. Every day Kate got a little better. At last she could go home.

Chapter 64

Kate knew a couple at church. Their daughter was a real estate agent. She called and asked them to have their daughter come to see her. The daughter did not come. Her husband did. He ignored Kate and asked Billie questions. Billie would say, "It's not my house. Ask my mother."

Then he would talk to Kate for a question or two and then he would turn back to Billie. The same thing happened at the doctor's office and at the hospital. Even though Kate was the one that needed help, people would question Billie or Elizabeth. Kate was mentally sound but at the doctor's office or hospital and now the realtor all seemed to think she couldn't answer the simplest questions. Kate was angry when he left. So she called Pat Franklin who also went to the same church as Kate.

Pat came out and talked to Kate. She mentioned a price, but Kate said, "That's too much for this little house. It only has one bathroom." So they decided on a price.

Kate had Billie call for a dumpster so they could begin to clean up the yard. During a break for lunch, Kate took Laren and Lance out to the Sizzler with Elizabeth and Billie. The two young men were her only grandchildren still living fairly close to Yucaipa. As Kate got rid of things, she invited both Laren and Lance to take anything they wanted, but only Lance came. The dumpster was filled and emptied and filled again. Billie loaded up the back of the pick-up and drove back to Flagstaff.

She went to Loyalton, an assisted living place and made arrangements so that when Kate's house sold she would have a place to live. Elizabeth stayed with Kate while Billie was gone.

After two weeks Elizabeth went back to South Dakota. Soon after she got home, Kate called Billie and said the last couple that had come over while Elizabeth was with her had bought the house. How things flew along. The house went through escrow without a hitch. The young couple was eager to move in. Billie went back to California to help Kate while she waited for the sale to become final.

So again Lance came out to get some things he wanted. He took the queen-size bed, the belt vibrator, the knocker that said Miller off the door, and many of the garden tools. Elizabeth had said that she wished she had a way to take home Mom's personal tool chest, so Billie decided to take it to her house for Elizabeth to pick up when she next drove to Flagstaff.

Billie called Julie in Flagstaff and had her go and tell the administration at Loyaton when Kate would arrive. So in the second week in October, Billie and Kate took off for Flagstaff. The tarp that was covering the goods kept blowing up into the air. Billie tried to tie it down but she just wasn't very successful. They had to stop several times for her to retie it.

They arrived at Loyalton on Kate's 92nd birthday. Julie had painted one of the beds from her children's bunk beds white with sunflowers. She had bought new sheets and towels and had the room all ready. Since the room was ready when they got to Flagstaff, Kate immediately moved into her room.

Billie unloaded the pick-up at her house and took Kate's things over a few things at a time. Julie and Andy helped. They took the two folding chairs, the television, Kate's clothes, her chest of drawers, and her rocking chair. They put pictures on the walls, and they bought her some fruit and seven-up.

Billie wrote letters to change the address of Kate's and Roy's retirement checks. She wrote to social security. She helped Kate open accounts at the bank and credit union. She wrote to the life insurance company. She closed her accounts in Yucaipa. She had her mail forwarded to her new address. She wrote a letter and sent it to everyone in Kate's address book. It read:

October 19, 2001

Katherine Miller
2100 S. Woodland Village Blvd. #106
Flagstaff, AZ 86001
928-779-2843

Hello All Kate's Friends and Relatives,

I am sending a generic letter to inform everyone of Kate's new situation. She has her own apartment in a lovely complex in Flagstaff. They all eat in a dining room and order from a couple of choices each meal. The food is good but not outstanding. There are lots of activities but she has not yet begun going to any of them but plans to sometime soon. She has walked up the stairs and up and down the halls getting acquainted with her new home, She has also walked around the building a few times. There are rocking chairs on the front porch and she has visited there a few times. There are sixty rooms and a few of them have two people in them. The sun is shining today. At night it gets down to about 30 degrees. During the day it gets up around 70 degrees.

She has spent quite a bit of time with me, her daughter, Billie and has seen her grandchild Julie and five of Julie's children.

She has been to a new doctor. Dr. Coats gave her a good bill of health and is having her blood checked on Tuesday. We have been busy changing her address, medical insurance, bank, direct deposits, and getting acclimated so it may be a while before she sends personal letters.

I ate lunch with her on her 92nd birthday and enjoyed the meal. They gave us small amounts but we had beef brisket and boiled cabbage that were quite good. They celebrated October birthdays on the 17th so Kate was there for that.

She can receive long distance calls but does not yet have a long distance carrier. She loves getting notes in the mail. I enjoy reading the letters to her, very much. Her address and phone number are at the top of this letter.

Best wishes,

Billie Banning

Kate then sent each of her children a check for $5000. She split Ann's $5000 between Pat and Erin. Billie used her money to put in a cement driveway.

Kate found that she was doing quite well at the home. She had been told that she could sit in any chair in the dining room. No one was allowed to save seats for friends. However, when she went down to eat, she was told time and again, 'That seat is taken.'

She did not want to sit where she was not wanted. She found that if she waited until lunch was half over she could find a seat. Then she found a place that was not taken by someone else so that is where she sat at every meal. She usually got more food than she wanted. Since she was not cooking she found that she ate much less than she had eaten when Roy was with her and she was fixing three meals a day. Kate stayed in her room much of the time. They had bingo and rummy and other games but Kate couldn't play because of her lack of sight.

Soon after she moved in she got another Braille player and the tapes began to come again. Now she could listen to the tapes as she stayed in her room. Billie went over daily and read mail since Herb was still cutting hair and she was retired. Occasionally, Herb and Billie would take her out to eat supper, but she really was not eager to go.

Mabel, her next door neighbor, had said "Shame on you." Kate had no idea why Mabel said that to her, but it bothered her a lot. Mabel played the games daily. Then she complained because Kate's tapes were too loud. One of the staff asked Kate to keep the sound down. If the sound was any lower she could not hear them so she quit playing the tapes after eight in the evening. It was too bad since often she would lay awake and she missed being able to listen to the stories. She went to Mary Beth, who had the room on the other side of her room, and they turned up her television as an experiment. Kate went back to her apartment and found she couldn't hear it at all. Mary Beth came over to listen, and she could not hear it either. Even after the little experiment, Kate did not listen to her tapes after eight o'clock.

Chapter 65

Billie once again asked Kate to go to church with her but Kate said, "No, I don't want to meet people with these ugly teeth."

When Billie realized that Kate would not go to meet new people until something was done about her teeth, she began asking people two questions: "Do you have a dentist you really like, and have you had quite a bit of dental work done?"

One day, Betsy Ann Suter answered 'yes' to both questions. Her son and husband both said they liked their dentist very much. So when Billie got back home she called their dentist, Mark Emshwiller, and made an appointment for Kate. She told his receptionist on the phone that Kate always had tears running down her cheeks whenever she went to a dentist.

The receptionist said, "Be sure and tell her that the first visit he will just x-ray and examine her teeth and it won't hurt at all."

Kate said, "It has nothing to do with pain." But on Tuesday she went to the dentist. She had x-rays taken and developed and then Dr. Emshwiller came in and sat down. "What would you like to have done to your teeth?"

Kate said, "When I hemorrhaged in California they put a tube down into my stomach through my mouth and broke off three of my teeth. They don't bother me. I can eat anything I want. But they are so ugly. So I wonder what my choices are."

The dentist answered, "Those three teeth need to be removed. There is no way they can be saved. So you can have all your teeth removed and put in a lower plate or you can have those three teeth removed and have a retainer put in around the four remaining teeth. The choice is up to you."

Kate asked, "Which would be cheaper?"

The dentist answered, "Both would cost a little less than $2000, so it would depend on what you want to do."

Kate asked, "If I get a lower plate would it click and clack?"

"Usually with a lower plate you need to use some kind of an adhesive to hold it in place. You are used to a retainer so just pulling the three teeth would be a little more like what you are used to," the dentist said.

"Tell me about the two choices," Kate said.

"If you get the three teeth pulled out, we will measure for a retainer before you have it done and you will walk out of here with a retainer the same day as we pull your teeth. If you get all your lower teeth pulled out you will come back when you have healed and we will put in a lower plate."

Kate asked, "You mean I don't get my lower plate until my gums heal. How long will that take?"

"It takes quite a while,"

"How long?" Kate asked.

"It's different for different people. It depends on how long it takes you to heal," the dentist answered.

Billie asked, "Are we talking about a month?"

Dr. Emshwiller replied, "At least. Some people take longer than that."

Kate said, "I live with sixty other people. I can't run around with no lower teeth for a month. I want the retainer."

The dentist said, "That will be easier on you too."

"When will we do it?"

"Make an appointment. We will make a mold for your retainer the same day we repair the three cavities in your other teeth. We will replace those fillings and you should be all set for about twenty years."

"I don't need anything that good. Probably five years would be long enough. I'm ninety-two."

"Well," the dentist smiled, "Let's just be on the safe side."

Billie said, "Mom usually cries when she goes to the dentist."

Kate added, "This is not my favorite place."

"I'm going to give you a prescription. You take one pill an hour before you come to my office next time."

So armed with the prescription they made an appointment for the next week and left. The pill worked well, and Kate was quite relaxed when she went back. The dentist filled her three cavities and made a mold which he said he would send to California. When the retainer was ready to be put in, they would call and have Kate come back and get her teeth pulled and the retainer put in.

Billie and Kate stopped at the Olive Garden on the way home. The soup and bread was wonderful. They had ordered a pasta lunch to split. That was a mistake as the soup and bread were quite satisfying, but they both ate a little of the pasta.

When the retainer came in, Billie was home with the flu, so Julie took her grandma to the dentist and had the three teeth pulled and the retainer put in. Kate was to take it out at night and put it back in the morning. But the next morning her mouth was much too sore.

Billie called the dentist and he said, "Just have her keep trying. Her gums are sore but she should be able to put the retainer in. I'll see her next Tuesday."

The next Tuesday when Kate went back to the dentist, she had a bad infection in her gums and had to take antibiotics to help them heal. It took over a week for her gums to heal enough so that she could start wearing her retainer, but finally she could.

Chapter 66

Friday night she was watching television and accidentally dropped the remote control. The batteries fell out. She tried and tried to get them back in but she just couldn't get it to work. After trying several minutes, she took the batteries and the remote control and headed down the hall

There were six people in front of the elevator. Kate thought one of them was a man. She walked up to him and said, "I really need a man."

How the people standing there laughed. It took her a minute to realize what they were laughing at.

She thrust the remote control and batteries at him and said, "I can't get it to work."

As soon as he realized what she wanted, he said, "Come on. Let's go to your room."

Again there was laughter. Kate turned toward her room. The young man followed her and his wife and an older woman followed him. He put the batteries in, tried it, and it worked fine.

Kate said, "Oh, thank you. I won't even kiss you. I'll let your wife do that."

His wife did and they left. Kate worried about what she had said, but Billie told her that it just gave the people at the elevator something to chuckle about.

Elizabeth and Frank came to visit Kate on their way to Quartzite, Arizona. They had another couple with them to share the driving. They had enjoyed the trip a lot as they had someone to drive and visit with. They were going to visit with a friend they all knew at Quartzite.

One of the pluses for Billie of having Kate live in Flagstaff was that people came to see Kate, so Billie saw a lot of nephews and cousins and other visitors that she would not have seen if Kate was still in California.

Kate was so happy because her grandson, Bob, and his wife, Marlys, and their three children; Dustin, Colton, and Rebecca came to see her. Dustin was roping in the national Rodeo in Farmington. Since they were that close to Flagstaff, they decided to drive over for the day. Kate so enjoyed visiting. She took them and Billie to the Sizzler. Right after the meal the Schaefers headed back to Farmington.

Dustin had won several state championships in South Dakota. He had won several belt buckles and a saddle and other things with his skills. He and his partner did not win the national championship but they did have a great week of camping out and watching the best rodeo people in the world in action.

Another of Kate's grandsons, Matt, was to be in Las Vegas because his boss had paid for the trip. Since Matt and Deb were within a day's drive of Flagstaff, they also came to see Kate. They stayed in the new addition to Billie and Herb's house.

Pat and Christopher came over from San Diego for weekend visits. One weekend in August, they came over to Flagstaff to visit Kate. They spent a night in a motel, then went to Kate's to visit, and then brought her over to Billie's for supper. Julie and her family came over, too. Before eating, everyone went up the steep steps to see the new second floor rooms. Kate went along and everyone was very careful of her. Pat walked up the stairs behind her so she couldn't fall. Then they ate supper.

After supper, Pat and Chris were taking Kate back to Loyalton, and then they were headed home. Kate was standing on the large top step outside Billie's front door. She stopped to admire the black metal silhouette on the step.

Billie said, "Lynn made her. That's Elizabeth and Ambree's shadow."

Kate said, "Lynn made this?"

"He sure did," Billie replied. "He also made the planter next to her. The flowers are not real. It's much too cold nights for real flowers."

After admiring the silhouette and planter, Kate forgot that she was on the top step and she stepped off into space and fell down the remaining step and cracked her head on the cement wall that was alongside of the walk.

Julie immediately ran into the house and came out with a couple of towels to hold against her bleeding head. Pat and Christopher helped her into their car. "We'll take her to the hospital."

Kate said, "You will not. You'll take me back to my room."

Billie said, "Mom, you need to go to the hospital."

Kate was adamant. "No way, I'm going back to my room."

As soon as they drove away, Julie said to Billie, "Mom, you need to call Loyalton and have them meet her at the door with a wheelchair."

As soon as she got off the phone, Billie headed to Loyalton.

When the trio got to the assisted living facility, Larry, Loyalton's 'jack of all trades' met them with a rolling chair from the dining room. "I couldn't find a wheelchair. Do you think this will work?"

Kate knew that if she didn't want to go to the hospital, she had to make it work. So she sat in the chair and they rolled her down to her room and to her bed.

A caregiver came and put a bandage on her bleeding head. She talked to Kate and again Kate said, "No hospital. I just want to go to sleep."

By the time she got into bed, Billie was there and gave her a Tylenol p.m. Pat and Christopher headed to San Diego, and Billie went home as soon as Kate went to sleep,

At 7:30 the next morning, Billie was back at Kate's door. Kate had been up, gone to the bathroom, taken a shower, gotten dressed, and was back in bed.

When she woke up and saw Billie, she said, "My hip hurts."

"I'm going to take you to the hospital," Billie replied.

"No, just take me to Dr. Coats."

But Billie knew that Dr. Coats did not have an x-ray machine so after negotiating with Kate, she took her to a walk-in clinic that did have one.

She borrowed a light canvas wheelchair from Kate's neighbor, Ardyce. They went to the clinic and an x-ray was taken.

The doctor said to Billie, "How did she get here?"

Billie said, "I brought her in my 1971 Chevy Impala."

The doctor and an assistant followed Billie and Kate out to the car. Very carefully, they put her back into the Impala,

Then the doctor said, "Here are the x-rays. She has a broken hip. She's tough. It's very important that the bones don't move. When you get to the hospital, you go in and have hospital staff take her into the hospital. I'm going to give them a call right now."

After Billie went in and told them that Kate was outside, two employees came out with a gurney.

Kate said, "I want a wheelchair. Not that thing."

Since she was insistent, they left and returned with a wheelchair. Eventually, she was admitted.

About two hours after she was taken to the emergency room, Dr. Durham came in where she was waiting in a bed.

He looked straight at Kate and said, "You have a broken hip." He was one of the few people that talked to Kate instead of Billie.

Kate asked, "What are you going to do about it?"

Dr. Durham said, "That's up to you. We can screw the two bones together or we can replace the hip."

"What's the difference?" Kate asked.

"The replacement will last a lot longer. The screws in the bones usually last six to eight years. Then we might have to do it again. It's up to you."

Kate said, "I'm 93 years old. Let's just screw my hip back together."

So they did. After the surgery, Kate woke up with vibrators on her legs. She also got a shot in her tummy to reduce the risk of blood clots.

When she regained consciousness, she found Margaret, a caregiver from Loyalton, taking care of her. "Have you quit Loyalton? Who's going to clean my room and change my sheets? When did you go to work here?"

The reply was, "I'm Margarita. That's my Mom that works at Loyalton."

After a few days, Kate was taken in a van to the Peaks. They were also an assisted living facility, but they had one wing that was for people recovering from surgery. She stayed there for five weeks. After a week, she would get up at night and use the bedside commode. By the second week, she would often push the commode into the bathroom and empty it. She couldn't believe that she had to empty her own commode but she didn't like having it by her bed after she had used it.

She shared a room with a woman. Whenever, she would push a button and a caregiver would come to the room, her roommate would call them, "I need help. I need help." Usually, after they were done helping the roommate they would leave without checking on Kate.

Billie said, "You could always call them and say, 'I need help. Please come and help me.'"

Kate said, "I'm not going to yell at them. They should know that I am here."

By the second week, Kate was taking showers alone. She went to therapy three times a week. She was to use her walker and not put any weight on her broken hip. It was very difficult.

After four weeks, she could move around pretty efficiently with her walker. It was time to go back to Loyalton. On the Thursday before Labor Day, Billie went to the desk to make arrangements to take her back on the following Tuesday. The woman at the desk said she would make the arrangements. Kate was a little nervous about going back to Loyalton over the holiday weekend.

Tuesday morning, about 8:30, Billie went to the Peaks. Kate had packed everything. She was ready to go back to her home. Billie went to the desk and asked what time the van was taking her back to Loyalton.

She was told, "No one has made those arrangements. Our vans are very busy. She won't be able to go there today. We have an opening for a van to take her back on Thursday."

Billie borrowed the phone. She called the cell phone number of the van driver from Loyalton. The driver, called Coach, answered the phone with, "I'll be right there to pick her up."

The woman was called Coach because she had retired from being a coach at Flagstaff high school. After she retired, she planned to supplement her income by coaching half the time at the high school. Then she heard about the van-driving job at Loyalton. The pay wasn't as good, but she thought she might enjoy it more.

When people asked her why she went to work at Loyalton, she answered, "At Flag High, I would have been the old lady. At Loyalton, I'm the young lady."

Billie walked down to Kate's room and told her Coach was on her way. She was as good as her word. Kate finished putting on her shoes and socks and Coach was there ready to take her back to Loyalton. They left and Billie went to the desk and checked her out.

Kate was glad to be back in her own room. How Margaret laughed when Kate told her that she thought Margaret was taking care of her when she was in the hospital. "That was my daughter, Margarita," she said.

Kate went to her meals in her rented wheelchair for the first six weeks. It was quite a distance to the dining room and using the wheelchair was the easiest. Around her room, she would use her walker. She tried to keep the weight on her arms instead of her left leg, but it was very difficult. She went to see Dr. Durham. Coach took her in the van so she could go in her wheelchair. He was very pleased at her progress. Soon she was walking down the hall with her walker, and the wheelchair just sat in her room.

In January, Billie called and asked the Northland Care Center to pick up the wheelchair. She left a message on the answering machine. In March, she called again. Again she got the answering machine. Then she got a bill for the chair. She wrote the check and enclosed a note asking them to pick up the chair. It was no longer in use and had not been used for four months.

A month later a young man came into Kate's room. He got the wheelchair and started to get Kate's walker. Kate stopped him by saying, "That's my walker. All you get is the wheelchair."

On January 6 of the following year, Billie got a hip replacement. Julie was wonderful about checking on Kate. It was fun to see her granddaughter. How Kate enjoyed her visits. Julie worked at a plant that enclosed medical supplies inside plastic. Most mornings she would work from 6:00 until 11:00. She would stop by on her way home. Even though it was lunch time, Julie seldom ate with Kate. She would explain, "I just don't feel like eating right after I get off work."

Julie and her friend from church, Vivian Drye, brought Billie beans and cornbread so that Herb did not need to prepare every meal. Everyone was surprised how well Herb took care of Billie. He fixed meals, helped her put on her socks and her support that she wore on her leg every night, and gave her any other help she asked for. She healed quickly.

A few days after Billie got out of the hospital, Elizabeth and Frank came through on their way to Quartzite. Elizabeth went over and spent the days with Kate. Herb and Frank watched TV. Billie rested and read. They ate Dinty Moore Beef Stew and pizza. A good time was had by all.

The day before Liz and Frank headed south, Kathy came and spent ten days. That was so nice for Herb. She took over the meal fixing and she also went and visited with Kate. Billie and Kate were very proud of their daughters and granddaughters. Julie had been looking after Kate, but this gave her a respite also. She was working quite a bit and she had a house and family to look after. Also, Pat came over to visit during that time. He came only on three day trips. He was very glad to be there at the same time as Kathy. Kate, Billie, and Kathy loved his company.

In May, Kate heard that Lynn and Gayanne were coming on Thursday. She went down on Wednesday and had her hair done. She wanted to look her best. Thursday, there was no Lynn. Friday, there was no Lynn. Kate said, "They probably got stuck in Las Vegas."

On Saturday, Gayanne called. They had gone to her son, K. C.'s wedding. Afterwards they had gone to visit friends in Fresno. Then they decided to wait until after Memorial Day to come over because of the holiday traffic. They were back at her daughter Lynda's house.

How wonderful when they came to visit! Kate enjoyed them so much. They all went over to Billie's house for one meal so that Julie and her clan could see and renew acquaintance with her Uncle Lynn and Aunt Gayanne. How Kate loved seeing her son and his wife, a couple of people that she loved very much.

After visiting Kate, they headed back to California. Lynn flew to Cabo San Lucas and met Pat McDonough. They went deep sea fishing and were very successful, though they released their catch. After all, they flew down there and couldn't take the fish with them. Then they went out in kayaks. They loved being in their little crafts on the gigantic ocean.

After their wonderful trip, Lynn went back to California to see his son, Laren get married. It was a great wedding and Laren had a special guest. He had been adopted. He had searched for and found his birth mother. She lived within fifty miles of him. She had given him up for adoption because she was so young and had muscular sclerosis. She had a cross around her neck with his birth date on it. She told Laren that she had a birthday cake for him every year. She came to the wedding and met Lynn, Gayanne, and Myra. She thanked them for raising her son so successfully.

Chapter 67

In June, after school was out, Billie started dropping off either Ambree or Elizabeth at Kate's once a week. The other one would go to weight watchers with Billie. Julie would get off work at 11:00. Then the five of them would eat a little. One time Ambree and Billie went by and bought two KFC dinners and they split them five ways. One time, they had white bread and butter and baloney and pluots, plums and apricots in one fruit. Sometimes they would go outside the dining room and sit at the tables, surrounded by the garden that Marie had supervised having the residents plant with flowers and vegetables.

Marie was the exercise lady, the party lady, and the garden lady. One day Kate found a radish by her sink.

She went looking for Marie. When she found her she said, "Did you put the radish in my room?"

Marie said, "Yes, I picked it from the garden."

Kate said, "Oh thank you. I enjoyed it so much with white bread and butter."

Marie was a dynamo. What the caregivers and Larry didn't do at Loyalton, Marie did. Kate thought she was the hardest working person she had ever seen. Marie was responsible for the activities and the happy hour every Friday afternoon. She was the diplomatic, friendly person that kept the people of Loyalton happy and busy.

After Kate got her teeth fixed she began going to the daily exercise class and also to the Bible classes three times a week. She went to many of the programs that Marie planned and implemented. Each year, Mrs. Hume's class from DeMiguel School came over and adopted a grandparent. Kate always enjoyed the pretend grandson. She was quite happy with her life in this assisted living facility. She was so thankful for the caregivers that cleaned her room and did her laundry. She loved Margaret, Marie, and Coach. She was as busy as she wanted to be and she enjoyed the beautiful backyard that had vegetables, strawberries, flowers, birds, and squirrels. It wasn't her home in Yucaipa, but it was home.

One day Kate was so excited. Her grandson, Laren was coming to visit. He was bringing his new wife and their two daughters.

Kate noticed that she had a rash on her back, but she didn't want to bother about it. After all, she had not seen Laren for a long time, and, besides, she did not want to bother with a little heat rash.

Laren and Leeann and the two girls came. It was a lovely visit and Kate was so glad they came. But her back felt like it was on fire, so as Laren's family went out to the car to go home, she had the nurse look at her back. The nurse took one look and said, "You have shingles. You need to go to the hospital and get something for them." It was a Sunday so nothing else was open. Kate got in her wheelchair and Billie took her out to the convertible. As Kate was getting into the front seat, Laren came over and put the chair in the trunk of the car, and asked where they were going.

When Billie explained, he said, "We'll follow you."

They went to the emergency room and he took the wheelchair out of the trunk. He made sure that they got inside all right and then off they went to California. It was a good thing Kate went when she did. The shingles began clearing up after Dr Johnson gave her a shot and a prescription. She never fully recovered from the shingles and always felt like she had a bad sunburn.

Unfortunately, the pin put in to hold Kate's broken hip together was grinding away at the bones and Kate was in lots of pain, so they went back to Dr. Durham. Dr. Durham told them that the way to take care of the problem was to replace the hip.

Kate said, "I'm too old."

Dr. Durham said, "I replaced a hip in a 104 year old and he is doing much better than he was before the operation,"

Kate said, "I guess I'll do it. I'll be like a lamb going in for the slaughter,"

Dr. Durham said, "I would have it done if I needed it. I think you will be happy that you had it done." He did replace the hip and he only took the money that Medicare paid to him.

After the operation, she went to the Peaks again. One day Billie went over and found that Kate's bell was so high that Billie could not reach it standing on her toes, so she couldn't have called for help if she needed it. Fortunately, she could walk with her walker almost immediately. After two weeks, she decided to go back to Loyalton.

A weekly event that Kate really enjoyed was the sing-along that was led by two women from the Bethel Baptist Church. They sang hymns and songs from the forties and fifties.

Two years in a row, Billie bought sixty triangles off the web. She took them to Loyalton and when the residents opened them, out would fly butterflies. Then Elizabeth and Ambree pasted out cookies and punch as the painted ladies flew around the patio. The second year, Marie had planted some plants the butterflies would like so that they would stay around longer.

Chapter 68

In October 2007, Billie took Kate to the eye doctor. She was getting where she could see very little. She had started counting the steps to the dining room because she knew that she seemed to lose a little more sight every day. Billie thought that maybe something could be done because there had been so much experimentation with macular degeneration.

Dr. McGarey told Kate they could do nothing about the macular degeneration but she needed cataract surgery in the worst way. So he operated on one eye on October 17 and the other eye November 28. He told Billie that she had the thickest cataracts he had ever seen. Kate was very happy. She could see better than she had been able to see for some time. She still had to turn her head to see, but she was quite happy to do that if it meant that she could see.

Kate was put on many pills. She was on Fosamax, and pills for blood pressure, and pills for cholesterol, and pills for acid reflex, and five other pills. She had never taken pills, and she found that these made her less alert and more forgetful. She talked more and more about her childhood.

She had lived at Loyalton for six years and ran out of money. Billie took many trips trying to get her on Evercare. The problem was she got quarterly checks. If the money was split so she got a third each month, she was not over the limit to get help. But the state of California would not send her the money monthly instead of quarterly. And Liz, at the Evercare office, would not let Kate sign up because every third month she got too much money. (Evercare was a part of AHCCCS for the elderly.)

Billie often went to Bible classes with Kate but one day she was too late, so she was sitting outside waiting for the class to end. While she was sitting there, a woman sat down and they got to talking. Billie explained about the quarterly check and the woman told her to go to legal aid and have them fill out a Miller's trust. That way the quarterly check would go to the state and she could then get on Evercare. That was just how it worked out.

Kate got ninety-four dollars a month to spend as she liked. Most of that went to get her hair done weekly. But most of her needs were met by Loyalton. Unfortunately, now that she was on Evercare, Loyalton was getting less money each month for Kate.

One day Kate said to Billie, "They are going to throw me out of Loyalton."

Billie was over there every day and she had the power of attorney so she thought that Kate had misunderstood something that was said to her.

Then Kate fell in the bathroom and she cut her arm quite badly. One of the caregivers found her bleeding in the bathroom and called an ambulance. At the hospital, the doctor, Julia Williams, explained that Kate's skin was too fragile to sew back together, so she taped it together, bandaged it, and sent Kate home.

When Kate got home, she began taking the bandage off. By the next morning, she had it off and was bleeding again. This time the caregiver called Billie. Billie took her back to Dr. Williams. This time she put on a much sturdier bandage. Both the doctor and Billie stressed that Kate had to leave the bandage on. They went back to Loyalton. Billie had to take Kate back to the hospital four times because Kate kept removing the bandage. The fourth time Dr. Williams put an Unna boot over the bandage. Then she suggested that Billie sign Kate up for hospice.

Billie said, "I don't think she is dying."

Dr. Williams said, "I think you should sign her up for hospice for your benefit more than for hers. They will help you to take care of her."

Billie took all the knives and scissors out of Kate's room so she couldn't cut the cast off. As she was leaving, the director, Gary Hughes, told her that she needed to move her mother to the nursing home, because she was too difficult to handle any more. He told her he had already sent the papers over there.

The next day, Billie went to the nursing home with a friend. Kate would need to share a room and bathroom. The rooms were very small and crowded. The box springs and mattresses were on the floor. People were sitting in the hall with their hands in their laps and their heads hanging down. She could see no activities going on.

She went to the desk and got Kate's papers. She showed them her power of attorney and they gave her the papers. It turned out that Gary had had Kate sign a paper saying that she would leave upon request way back in March, so Kate had been right when she said they were going to throw her out of Loyalton. Billie was furious. Gary had no right talking to Kate without also talking to Billie.

Billie wrote a letter to the parent company: It read;

Emeritus Assisted Living
3131 Elliot Ave., suite 500
Seattle, WA 98121-1031

Dear Person,

My mother, Katherine Miller, was a resident at Loyalton in Flagstaff from October 2001 to June 2007. It is a wonderful facility. A large part of this is the many activities planned by Marie Pickle. The care givers were very nice and friendly and helpful to my mother.

My mother sold her house and was on private pay until the end of 2006. At that time she went on AHCCCS.

When the first room that my mother was in became part of the special care wing, she was instructed to move to another room. Her family did all the moving. Even though she had been at Loyalton for three years and was 95 years old, she was moved very far from the dining room. She had had a broken hip and it was very painful.

My mother had hip surgery that was not successful. She bought an electric wheelchair. She and I worked hard to help her to learn to ride in it correctly. Gary was very reassuring as we took the wheelchair around the facility. Loyalton had the paper that showed that I had Katherine's power of attorney. The day I left on vacation, Gary instructed my daughter in very unfriendly and rude terms to take that wheelchair home before Kate ran over someone.

The next year when I went on vacation (Mom had had her hip replaced and was doing much better) Gary stopped my daughter in the hall and said, "Kate is a trouble maker and something needs to be done about it." My daughter was flabbergasted and I can tell you that that statement was untrue. Gary never said anything unfriendly to me and I was there at least five days a week.

My Mother could not see very well. She had macular degeneration and cataracts. So the activities she enjoyed most were the Bible classes and exercise with Marie. One day after a Bible class, my Mom hurried across the hall to the bathroom. When you are 96 years old, sometimes you are given very little notice. As she was going, Gary opened the door. When he saw my Mother, instead of quickly closing the door as any normal person would do, he stood in the open doorway and scolded her for not locking the door. She felt very humiliated.

In March of 2007 my Mother became very unsure of herself. She kept telling me that they were going to throw her out of Loyalton. I said, "Of course they won't, Mother. Why would they?" She said, "Gary doesn't like me." She did become very agitated and began roaming around at night. In May she fell and scraped her skin on her arm and bled a lot. I was called at 6 a.m. I suggested that they call an ambulance as there was a lot of blood. Her arm was bandaged and I returned her to Loyalton. The next week she took off her bandage every day. After the fourth visit to the hospital (I took her each time except once) Dr Julia Williams put on the bandage and then enclosed it in a cast. This made it impossible for Mom to take off the bandage. She also had me sign up for hospice. The next day, as we sat in the foyer of Loyalton, waiting for the ladies of hospice to show up, Gary called me into the office and said I was to remove Mom from Loyalton. I got the signed letter in the mail the next day. My mother had signed it back in March. Why was nothing said to me at that time? I think Gary frightened my Mom and if he did it to her, he did it to others.

I said, "Let's put her in the other wing."

Gary said, "There is no room."

I said, "She has been here six years. It seems like you could have moved her in the past few months when there was room. I know of three ladies that had moved there very recently."

Gary said, "Most people only live in a home like this for three years."

I found that he had already sent my mother's folder to the nursing home in Flagstaff.

Again I say, I was there 5 or 6 times a week. I taught the Bible class Saturday mornings. Mother and I had several friends in Loyalton. Many people in the other wing were friends of Mom's. She would have been quite happy there.

Since Loyalton is such a nice facility, Gary might be quite good at his office job. But he is a man who has no respect, no compassion, and no empathy for these old people and their families. My suggestion to you is that he never is to speak to any residents except to say 'hello' and 'have a nice day'. It is obvious to me that his feeling for these adults that have given up their homes is very unprofessional. Both Sandy and Sherrie were kind and understanding. Perhaps they should deal with the residents and families. And I am sure that whoever is in charge should speak to the person with respect.

Sincerely,

Billie Banning

Signing Kate up for hospice turned out to be a blessing. Barbara from hospice told Billie that they had opened a new house and it had room for her mom, so Kate was moved to a beautiful house on a steep hill by the Country Club. She had a large bedroom with two beds, but it had just opened so she had the room all to herself.

One problem was that the caregiver was a 40-year-old man from Ghana, Africa. His name was Obed. He had been in the United States for eleven years. Kate hated having a black man help her dress so Billie went over there every morning and evening to help her dress and undress. Carolyn from hospice came and gave her a shower twice a week. Obed was a hard worker and the meals were good and the house was very clean.

There were no activities but Billie went over every morning to help her dress and stayed three or four hours. Most of that time they sat on the balcony in a beautiful neighborhood. While they visited, Kate told Billie about her childhood and the early years when Billie was young.

Kate did have her books on tape and hospice volunteers went by and visited with her three or four times a week. While there, Kate became an escape artist. Obed ended up putting locks on all the doors and they had to be opened with a key on the inside as well as the outside. There were chimes on all the doors so if a door opened Obed knew it. He only had three people that he cared for.

Still, Kate kept him on his toes. One time she climbed over the rail of the balcony. In the front, it was on the second story, but the backyard was as high as the balcony. So Kate climbed the rail and walked around in the backyard, but there was no way she could get out of the yard. Eventually, Obed let her come into the house through the patio doors.

A couple of times she did get through a door that was left open, but she had to go down ten steps and then down a very steep driveway. The steps were hard to negotiate with her walker, so she was always found before she got down the steps.

One of the other residents was named Harold. One day, Harold's son came over to get him for an outing. As they were leaving, the son saw Kate walking down the street. He had no idea how she got away from the house. He called Obed and told him. Obed jumped in his car and went to get her. She was wearing out, so she willingly got in his car, and they went back to the house.

As a result of that escape, she was asked to leave the House in the Pines. Fortunately, they had room for her at the Ranch. It was about ten miles from Billie's house and it was on Easy Street. Billie just had to chuckle because Kate was ninety-seven years old and she was still one feisty woman.

Meanwhile, Billie and Herb had decided to remodel the bathroom. When Ida, Herb's mother, stayed with them she had to take sponge baths because she could not get into the tub that was eighteen inches higher than any other tub. They had decided to have it replaced with a walk-in tub, so a salesman came to call. He told them that he could put in a tub for $15,445. Because of the price, they decided to rip out the tub and put in a shower instead. They called several contractors and finally found one that was willing to work on a project as small as a bathroom. They bought the shower and the cabinets and the sinks at Home Depot and it still took three workers over a month to complete.

Kate moved to the Ranch. It was north of Flagstaff off of highway 89 which went to Page. The Ranch was a large house. It had two bathrooms but they were both rather hidden. Kate was in a large bedroom with another woman. They gave Kate another pill as well as all her others. This one was to help her make the transition to another place.

At the Ranch, she rapidly went downhill. She could not find the bathrooms. She would get lost trying to find her bed, so she climbed into any bed she could find. She got more and more lethargic. Billie told the woman in charge of the Ranch that when the month was up, she was going to take Kate home. She would not live there in September.

On August 11, Billie got a phone call from the woman at the Ranch. She said that Kate was quite ill and they had called, Kelly, the hospice nurse. Billie called Kelly's cell phone and told her that she was on her way out.

But Kelly said, "I'm just pulling into the yard. I'll call you as soon as I've seen her."

So Billie waited by the phone. Kelly called, "She is quite ill. I can't believe how much she has gone downhill these last four months."

Billie asked if Kate would be able to walk out and get into a car. Kelly didn't think she could. So Billie and Herb talked it over. They went upstairs and brought down the twin bed. Then Billie called Julie and Andy and asked if they would go with her to get Kate and all her things.

So about thirty minutes after Kelly's phone call, they were headed in two cars out to get Kate. Andy had to carry Kate to Billie's pickup, because she was so weak.

The woman at the Ranch wanted to know what Kelly had said about the Ranch. Billie told her that Kelly had said that she thought Kate was dying, so Billie decided to get Kate so she would be with her when that happened.

They loaded everything into the vehicles and drove to Billie's house. Kate saw the bed in the dining room and said, "You have me out here in front of everybody."

Billie said, "You've been lying around so much we thought you might like being out here with us. That way if someone comes, you can decide if you want to get up or not. We will be very glad to move your bed into our bedroom. We have plenty of room in there."

"No," Kate said. "I think I will like it here,"

Andy put high locks on all the outside doors so Kate could not open any of the doors and go outside or into the garage. It was a good thing because each of the doors was opened the inch that the lock allowed at different times, so Billie knew that Kate did sometimes try to open them. Billie put a walker on each side of the bed because Kate would go to bed on one side and get up on the other. Billie and Herb always left the bathroom light on so Kate could find her way.

When Laura, another hospice nurse, came, Billie said, "How do you feel if I take her off all these pills except the one for acid reflex and the one a day vitamin?"

Laura said, "You don't have to give her the vitamin if you don't want to."

So the pills were discontinued. Soon Kate was eating an egg and a piece of toast for breakfast. Sometimes she had a slice of bacon. Billie couldn't believe how much she improved. Soon she was going to Silver Sneakers with Billie and three other seniors that Billie picked up. She also started going to Bible study with Billie.

Laura came one day when Ambree, Elizabeth, Billie and Kate were taking the seeds out of a pumpkin to make a jack-o-lantern. She said, "I just love coming here as my last stop. You are always so happy."

That year for Christmas, Julie and her family slept in Billie and Herb's upstairs. Billie and Herb had lots of Christmas decorations and Julie brought all their children's gifts over so they could open them in front of their great grandma. Kate sat in her reclining loveseat and watched the children open their gifts. It was a very exciting Christmas for her. The children made cinnamon rolls and everyone had several rolls and drank coffee or milk. About 10 a.m. Julie and Andy took their family home. It had been a very exciting four hours.

Billie had bought a turkey dinner for six from Safeway. Herb, Billie and Kate ate lunch about two in the afternoon. Then they watched *It's a Wonderful Life* on television.

When Kate went to bed, she said, "It has been a wonderful day."

On December 28, 2007, Kate did not want to eat. Billie made her some oatmeal and she ate a little. Billie called Laura and asked her to come over. Laura came and talked to Kate a little. She was sitting on her loveseat. Laura asked her if she wanted to go lie down but Kate said, "No."

She asked if Kate wanted to stay on the loveseat and Kate nodded.

The nurse took Billie to one side and said, "Don't try to feed her anymore. She is shutting down."

So Billie made calls to Julie, Kathy, Elizabeth, Lynn, Pat and Erin. Julie and her family came over to sit with Billie. Someone held Kate's hand and talked to her throughout the day. About 6:00 p.m. Julie said, "She's gone, Mom."

Billie called Laura and then the mortuary. Both came to the house quite quickly. They wrapped her in red velvet and took her away. Billie had made arrangements to have her cremated.

Early in 2007, Billie and Lynn had decided they should have a family reunion while Kate was still alive. Arrangements had been made to have it in July of 2008. Now Billie decided that since she was going to be cremated, she would have a memorial service at the reunion.

The memorial service was on Sunday. The children and grandchildren told Grandma Stories. Erin said the line that every person heard when they called Kate on the phone, "What do you know that I don't know that I should know?" and Pat sang a song he wrote. The chorus was:

Roy and Kate in heaven are smiling down upon you,
Watching and helping with their love
Roy and Kate in heaven are smiling down upon us,
Remember who loves you from above.

Kate went to heaven on December 28, 2007.

Made in the USA
Charleston, SC
19 September 2013